Happy [illegible]ster

Color me

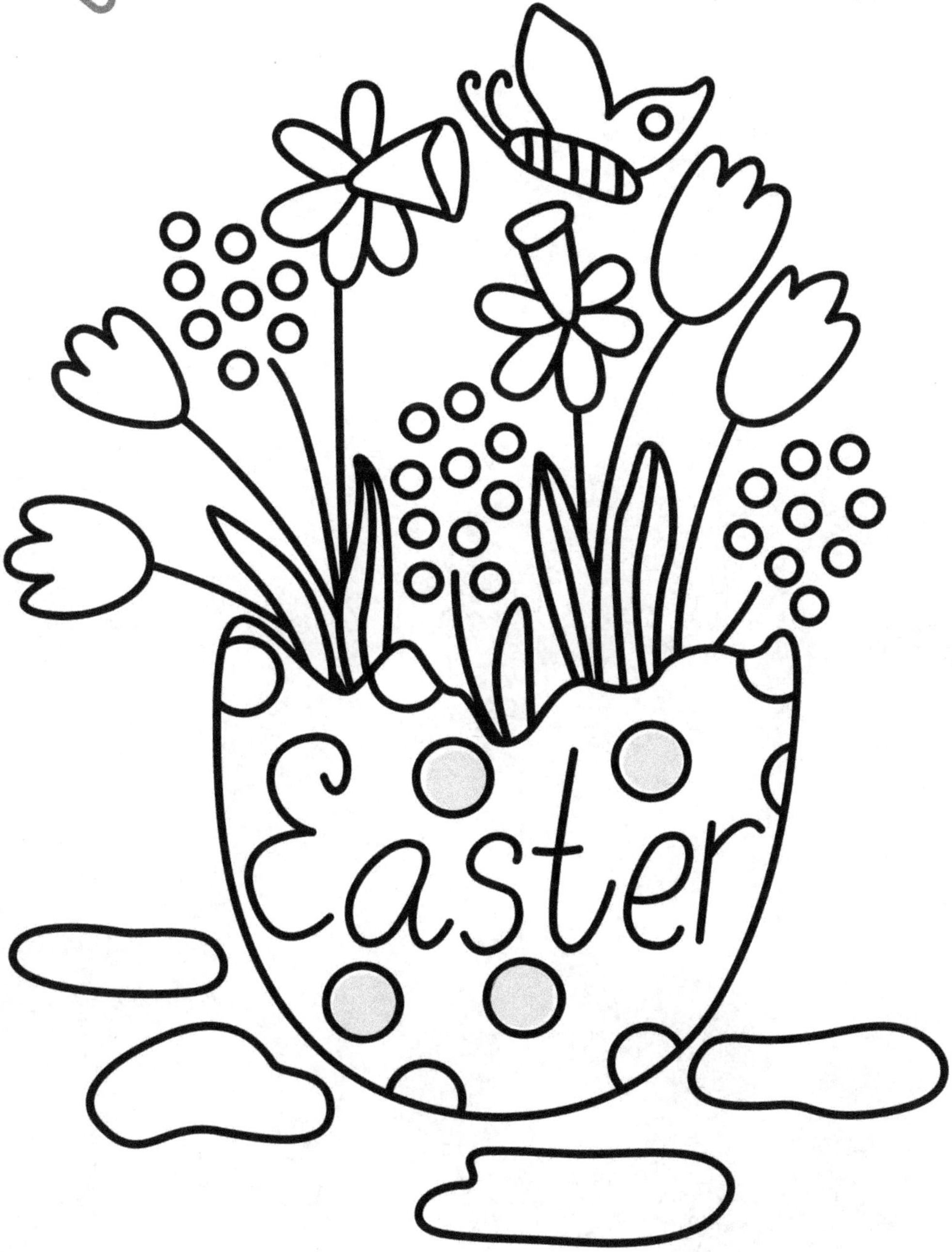

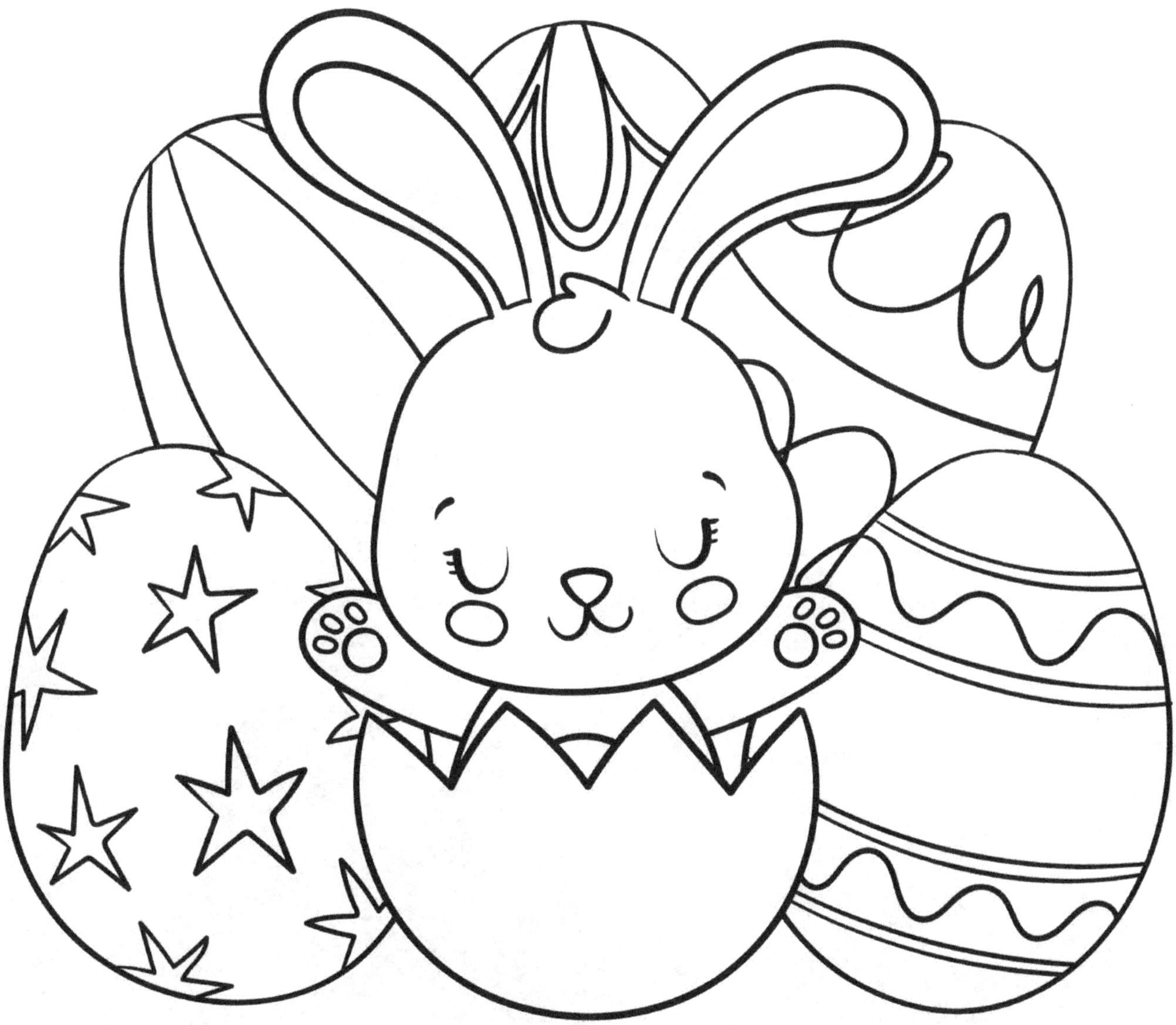

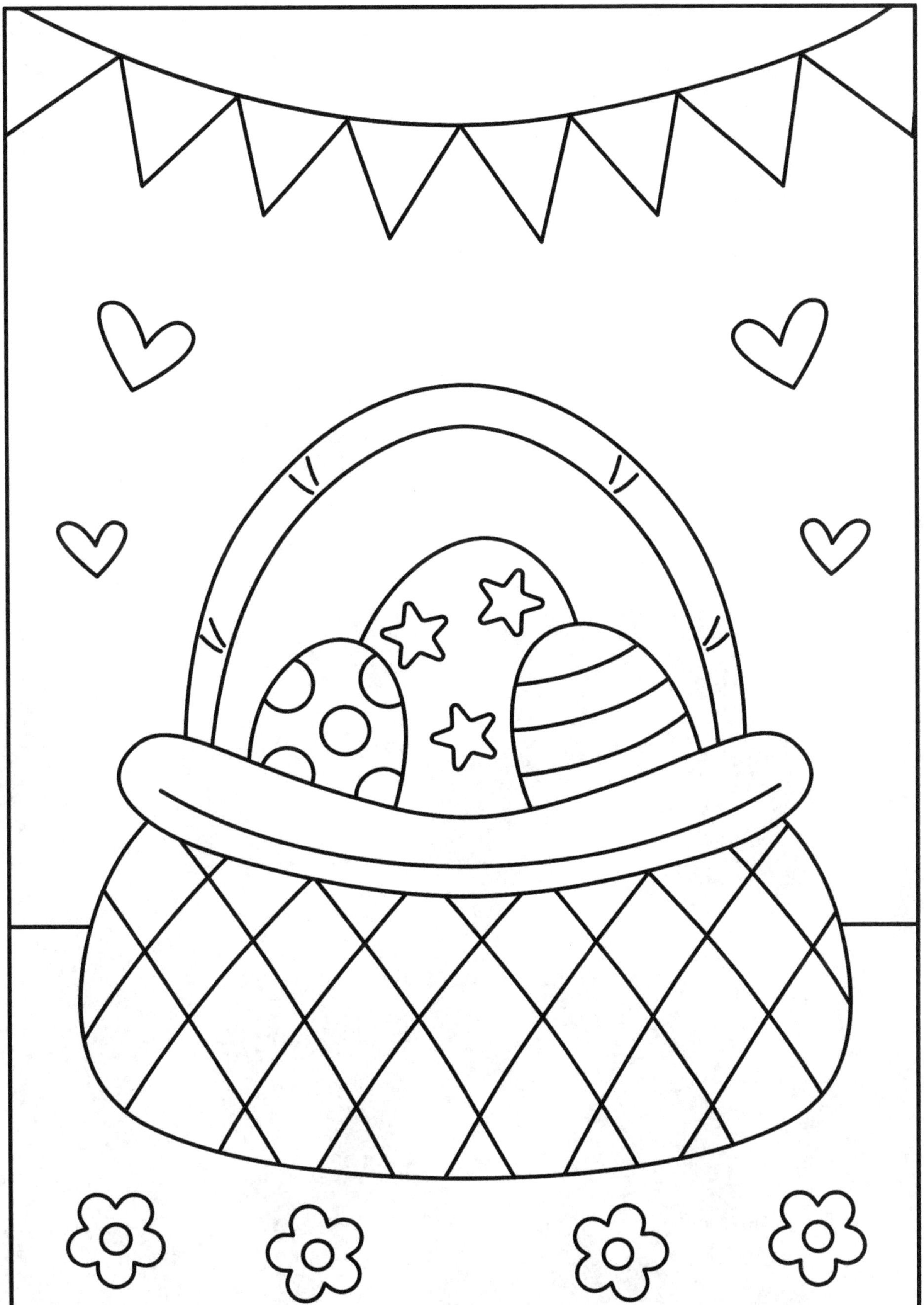

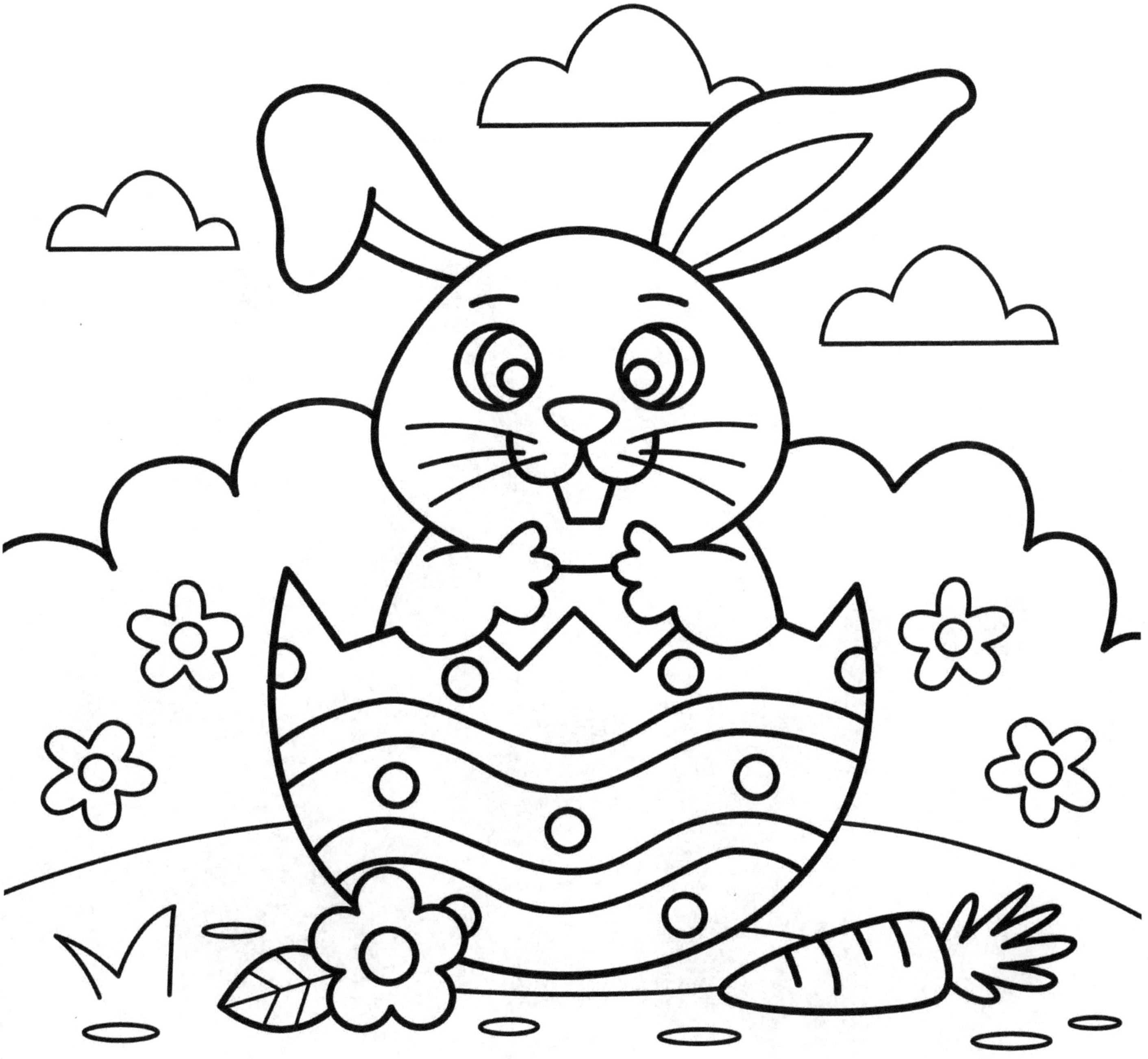

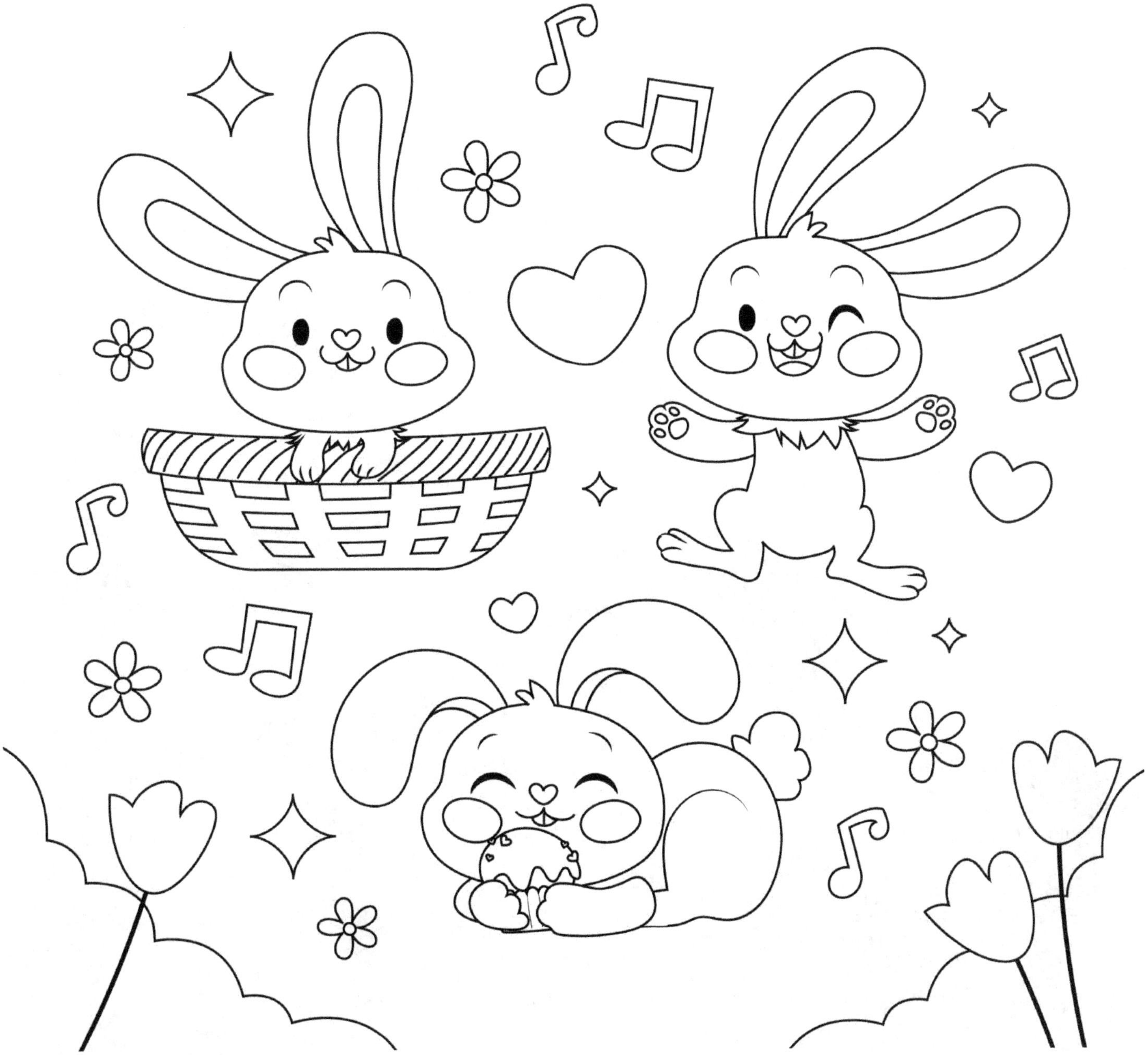

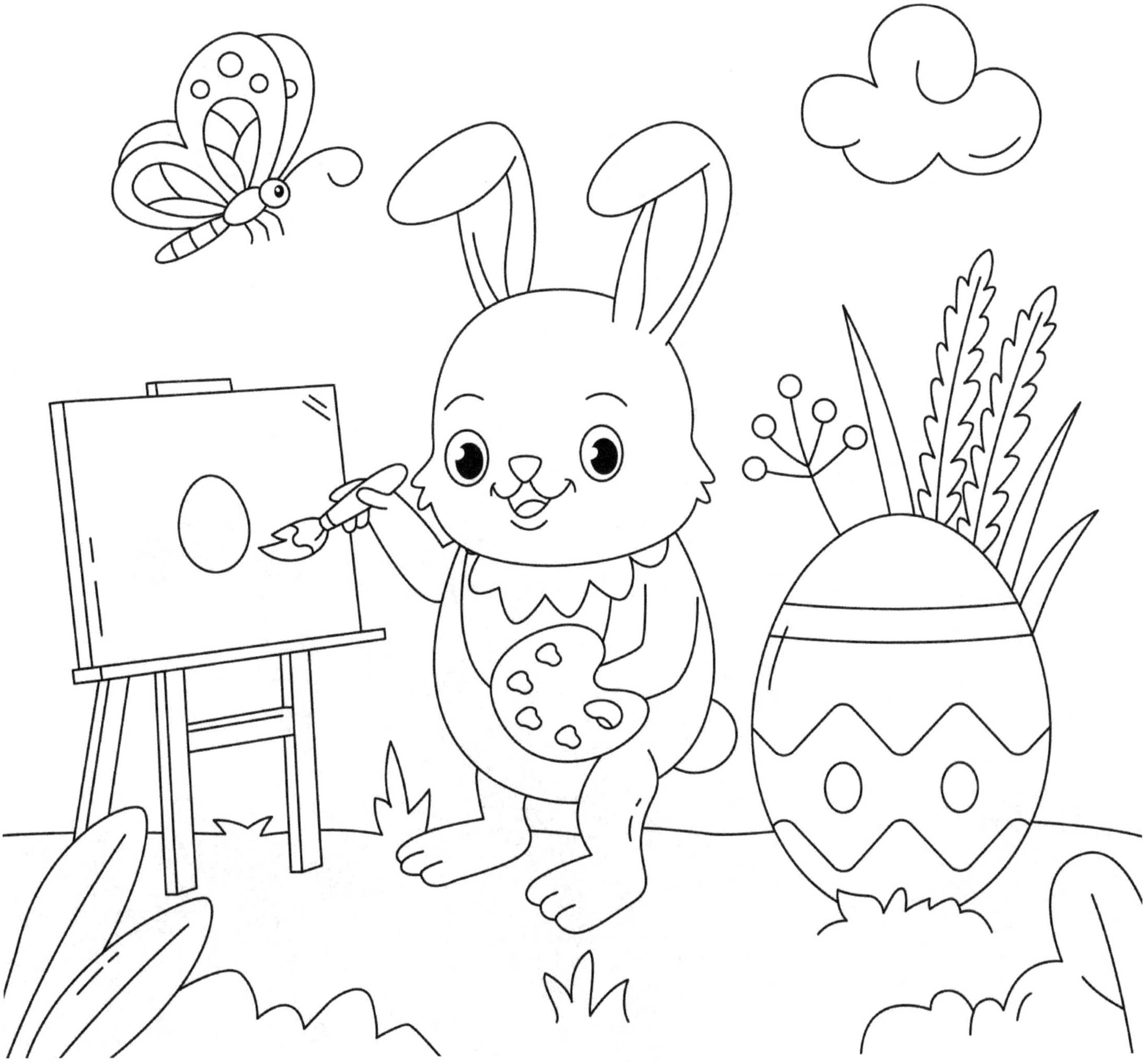

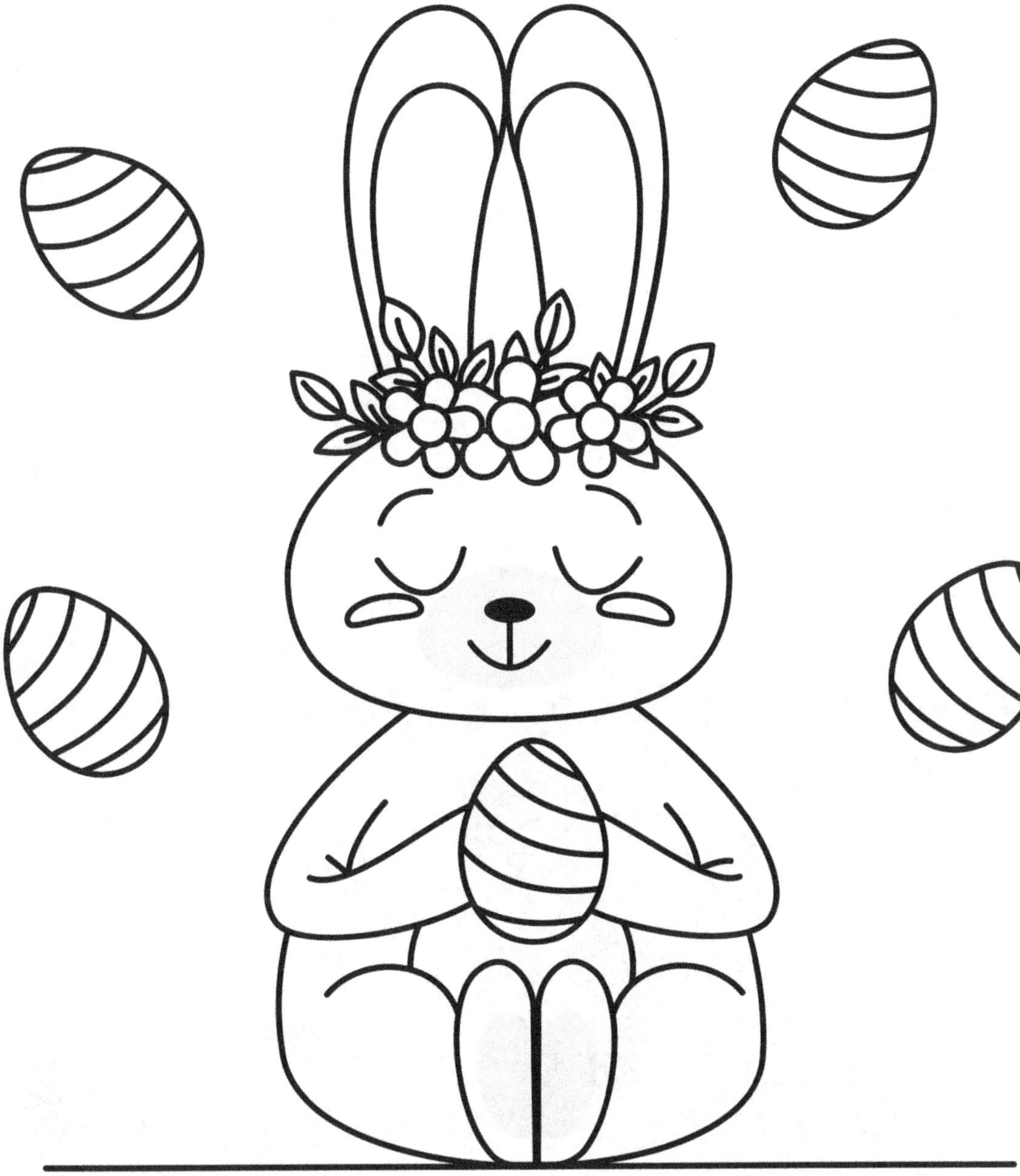

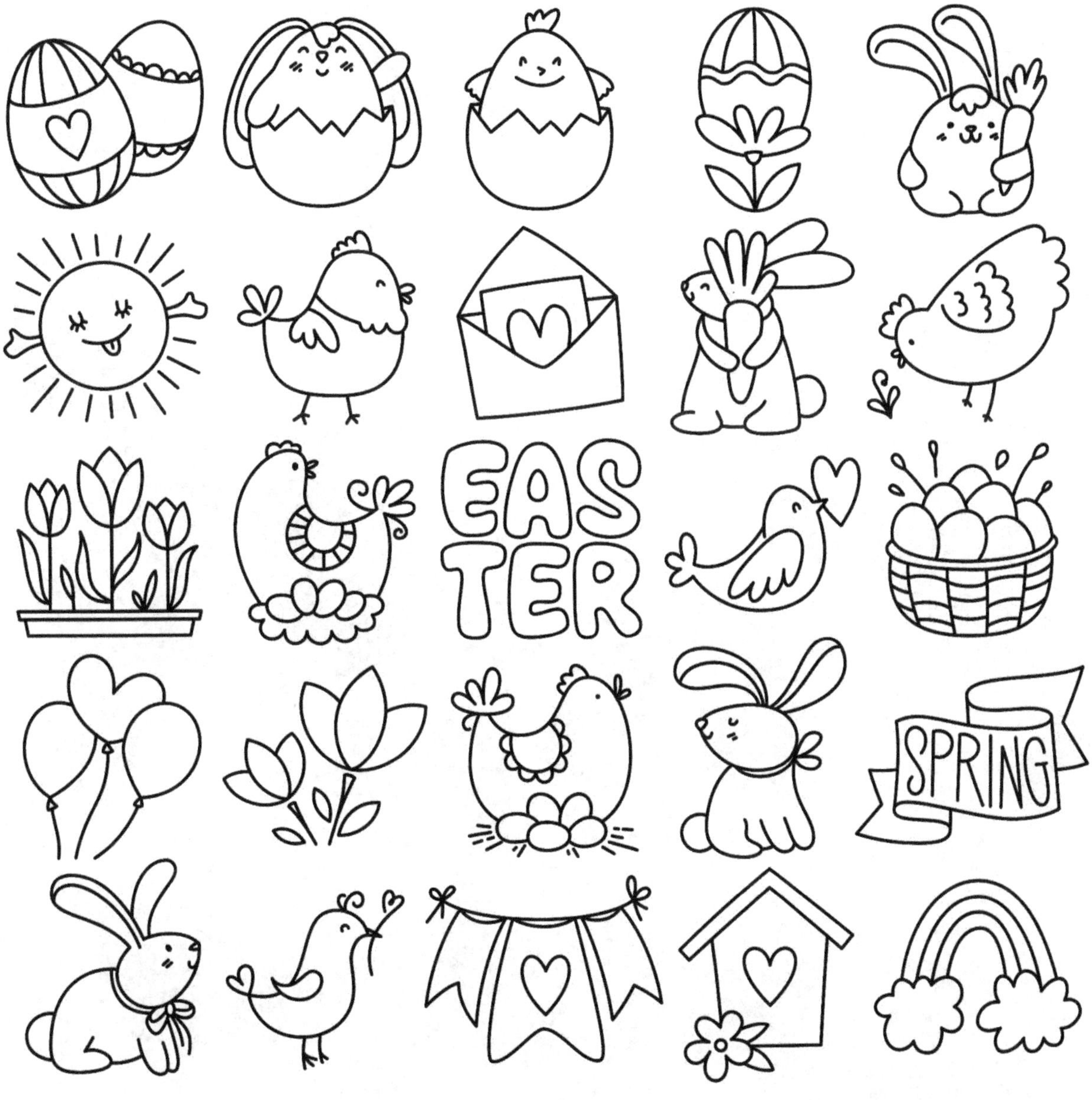
EAS
TER
SPRING

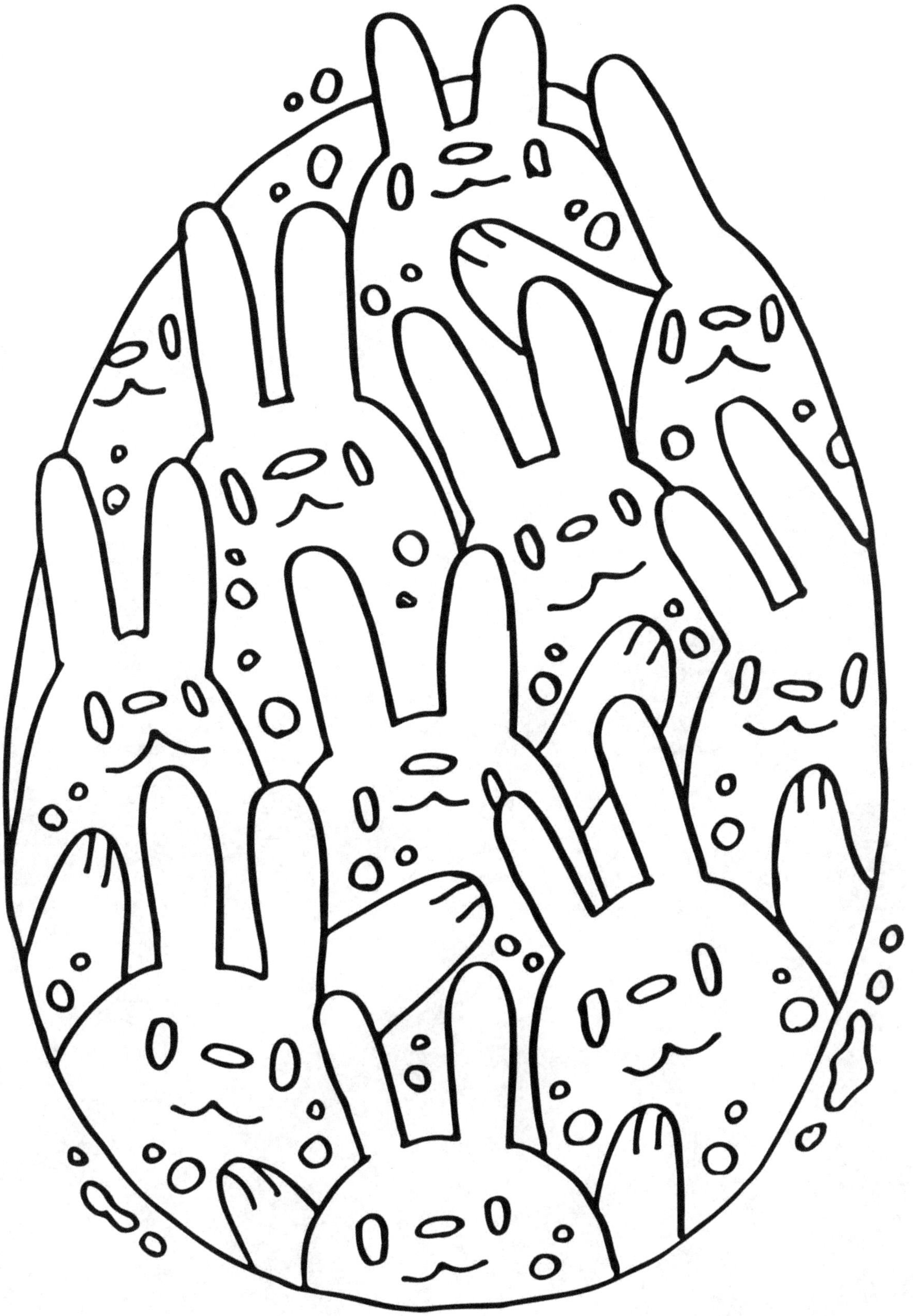

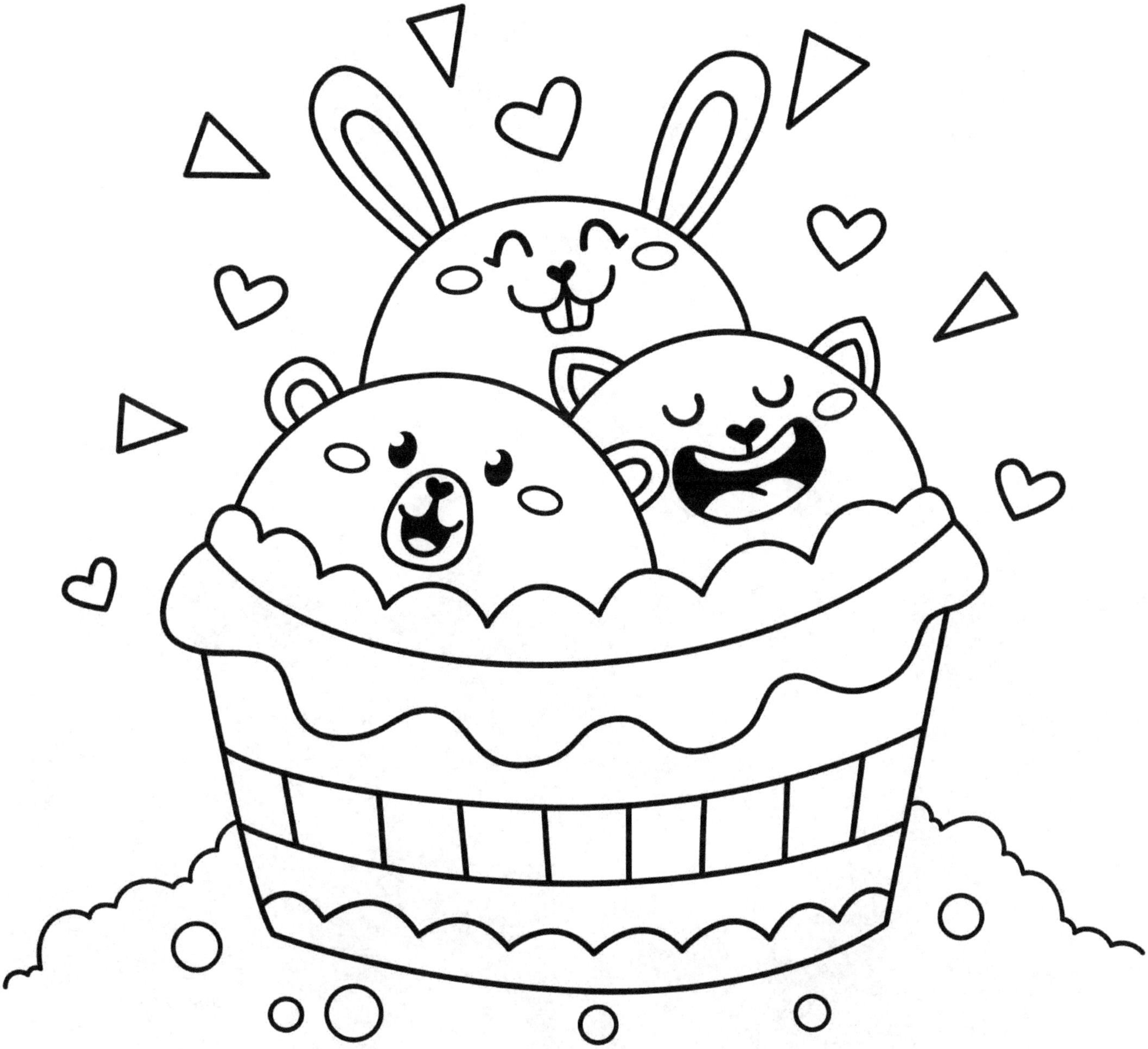

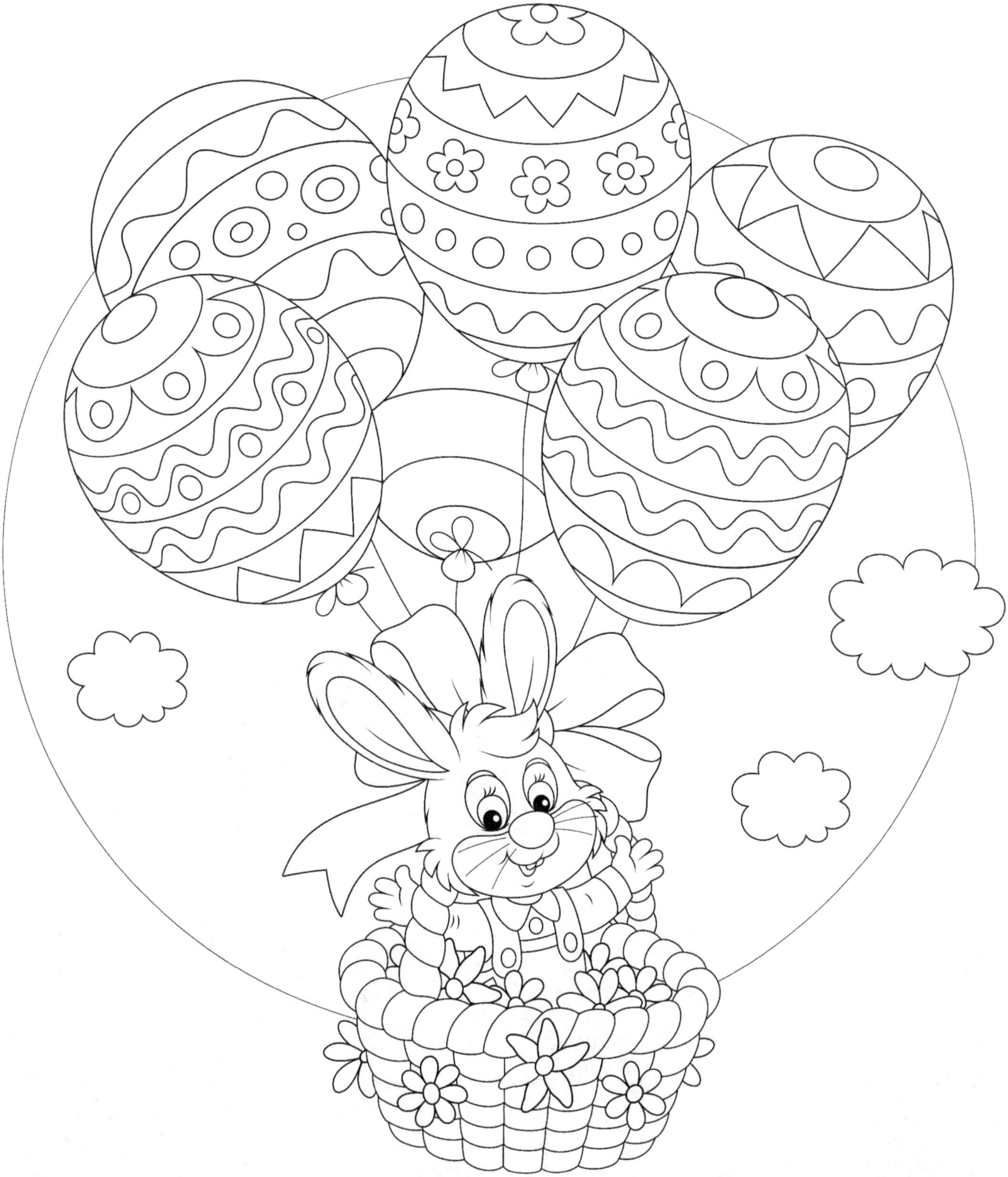

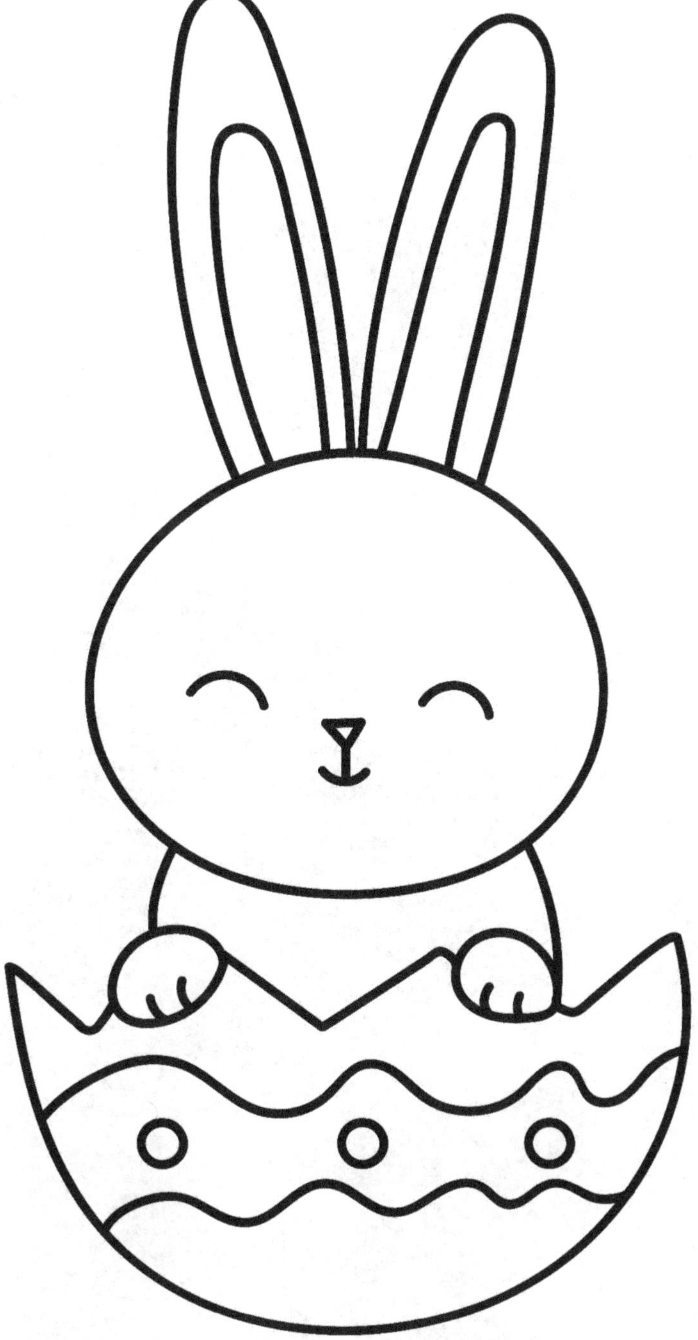

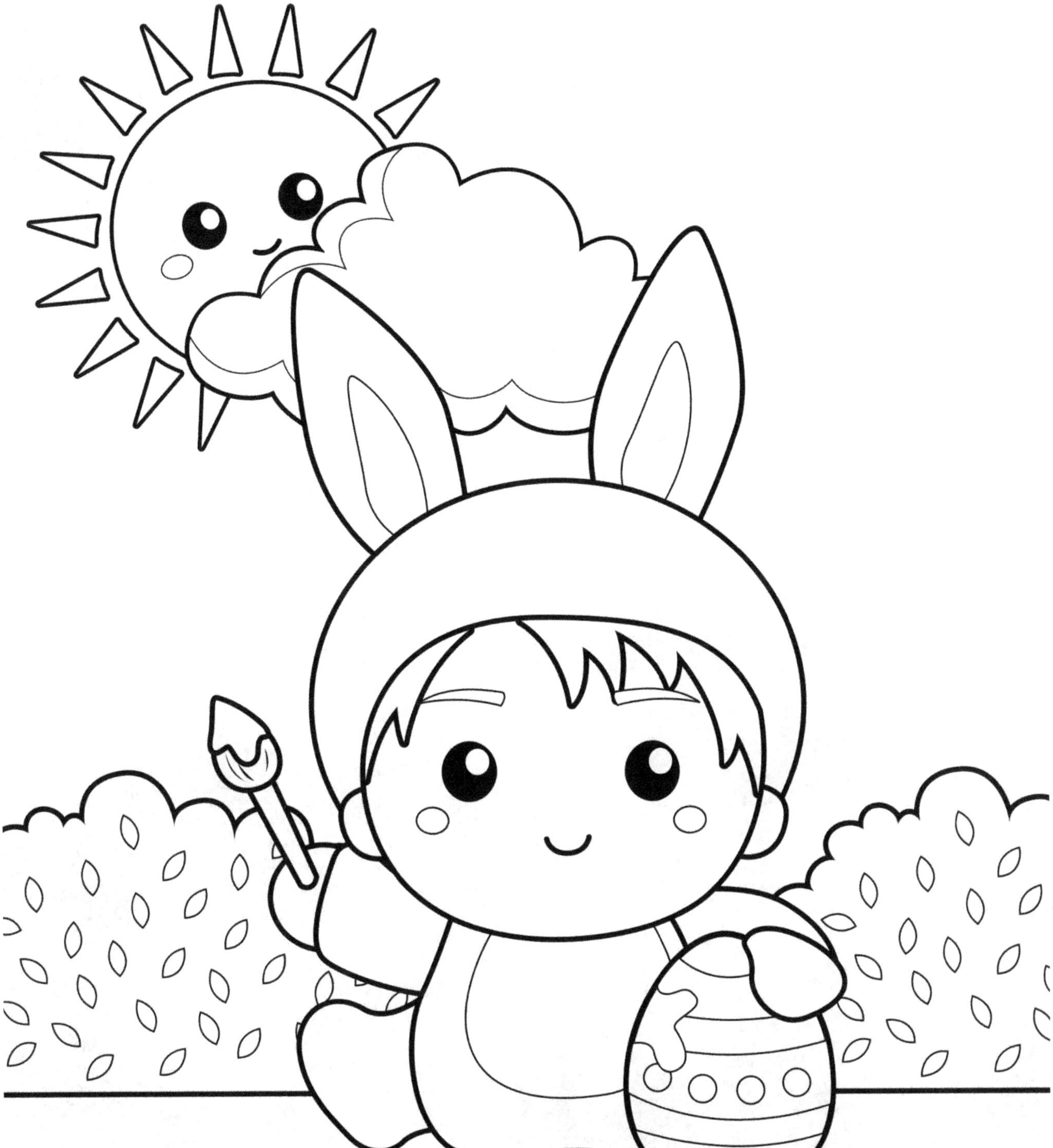

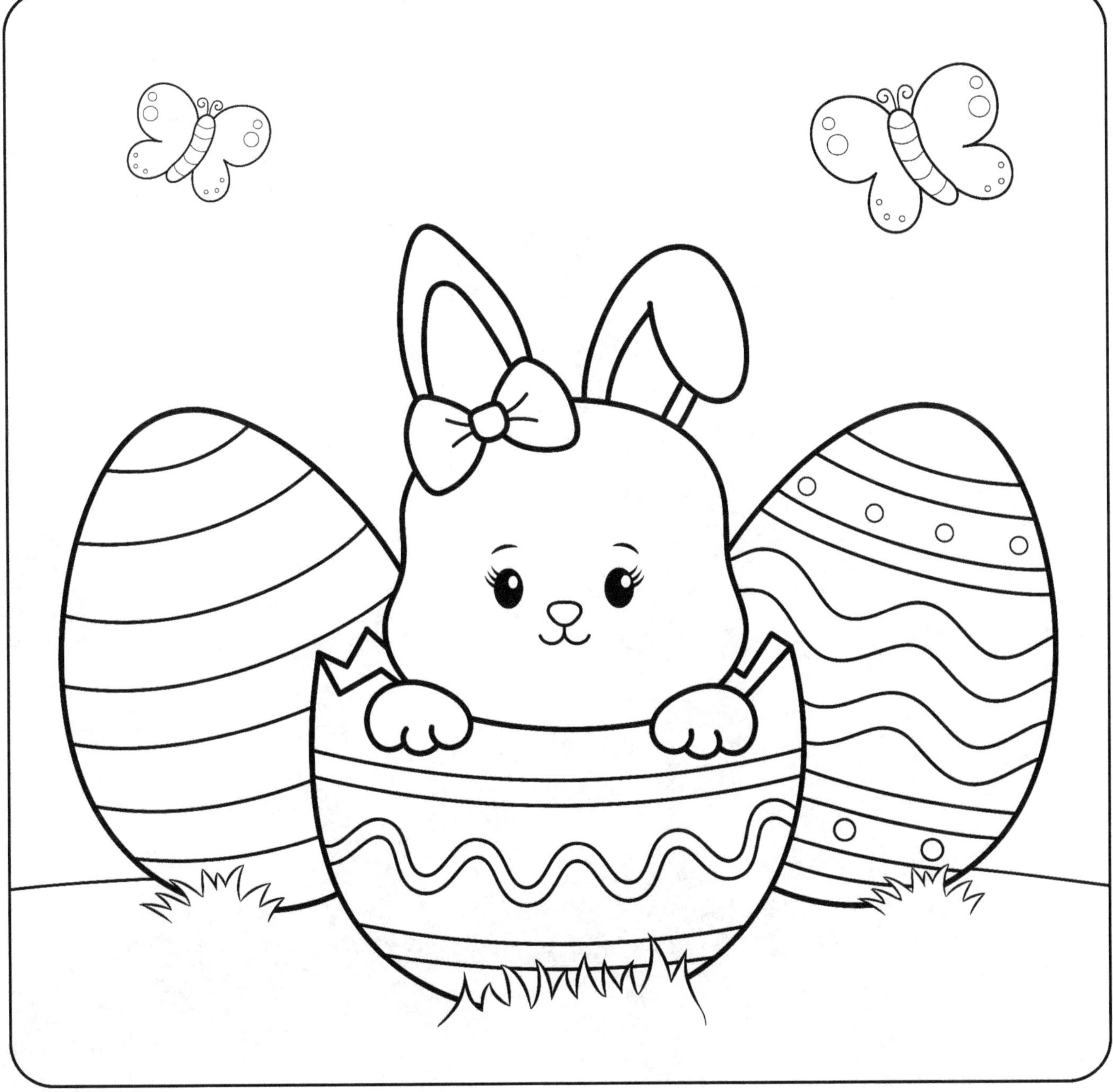

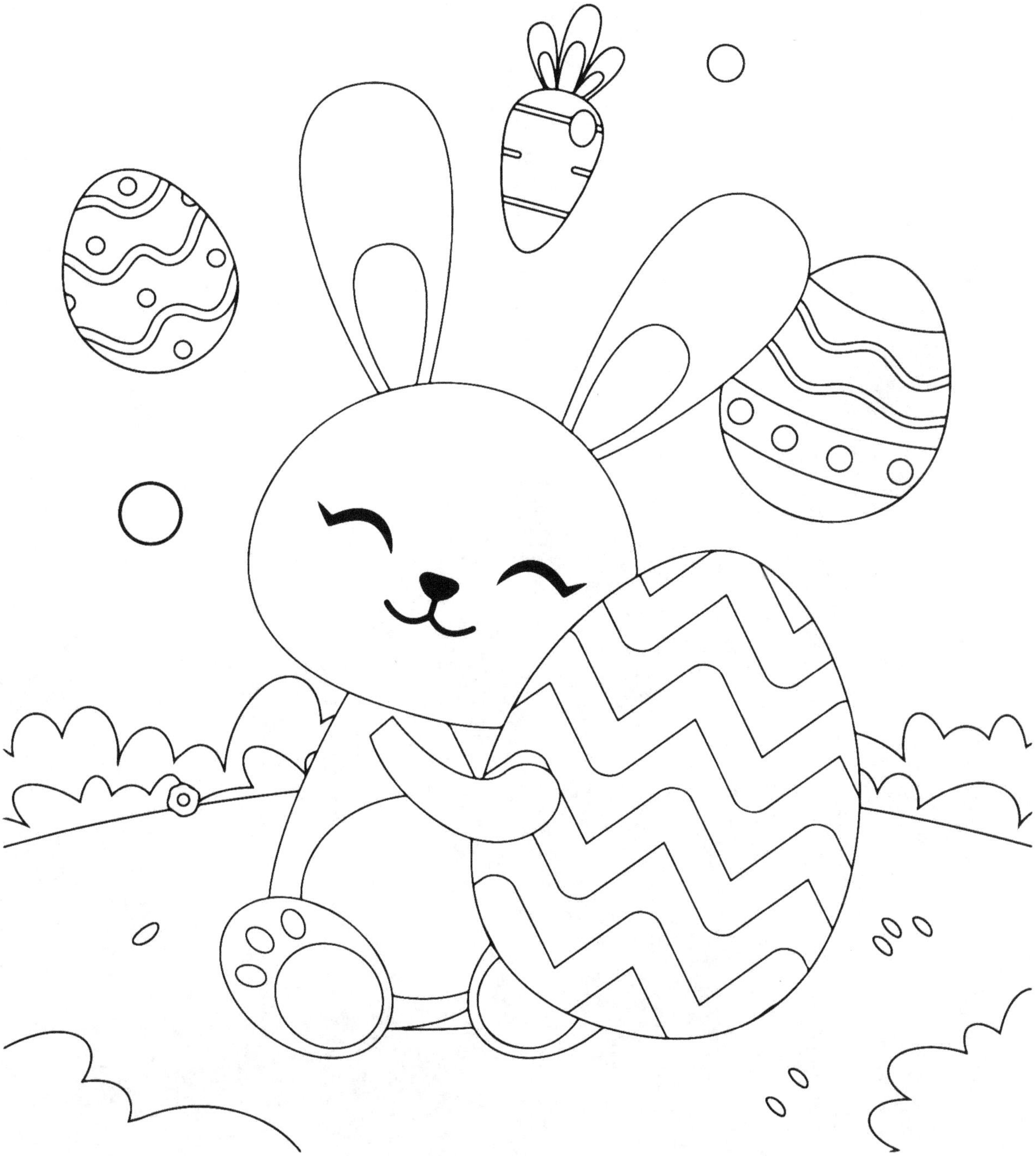

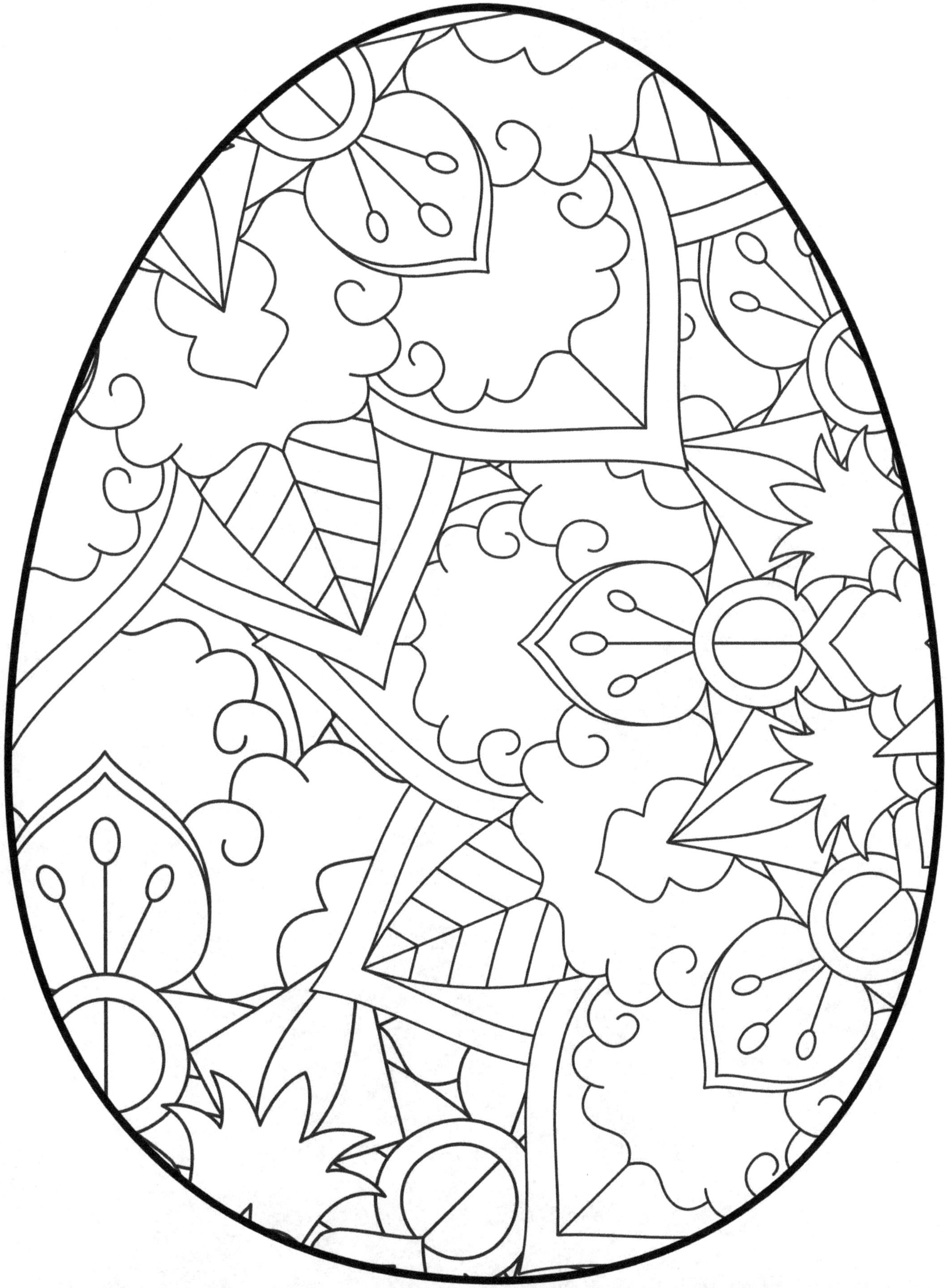

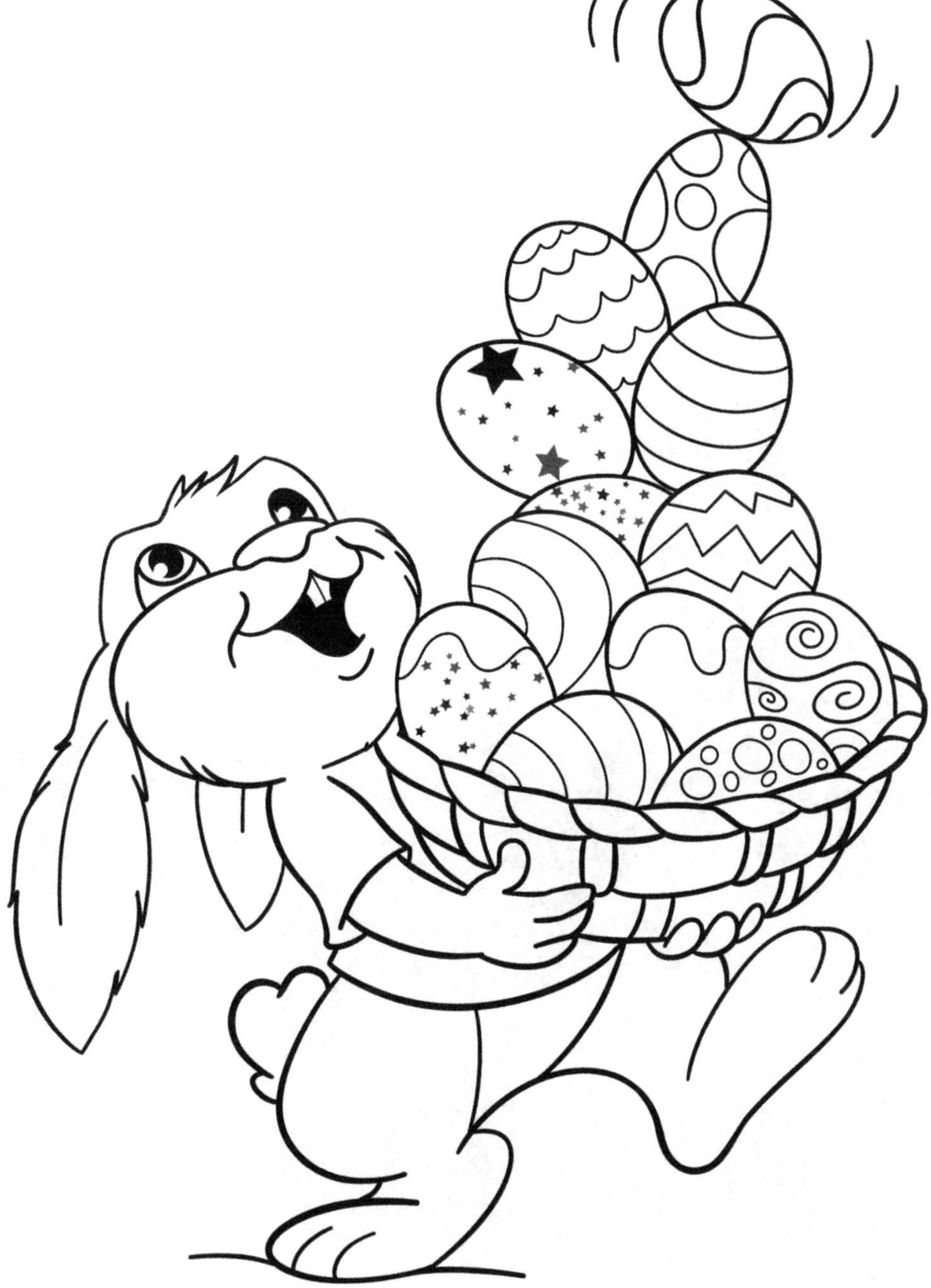

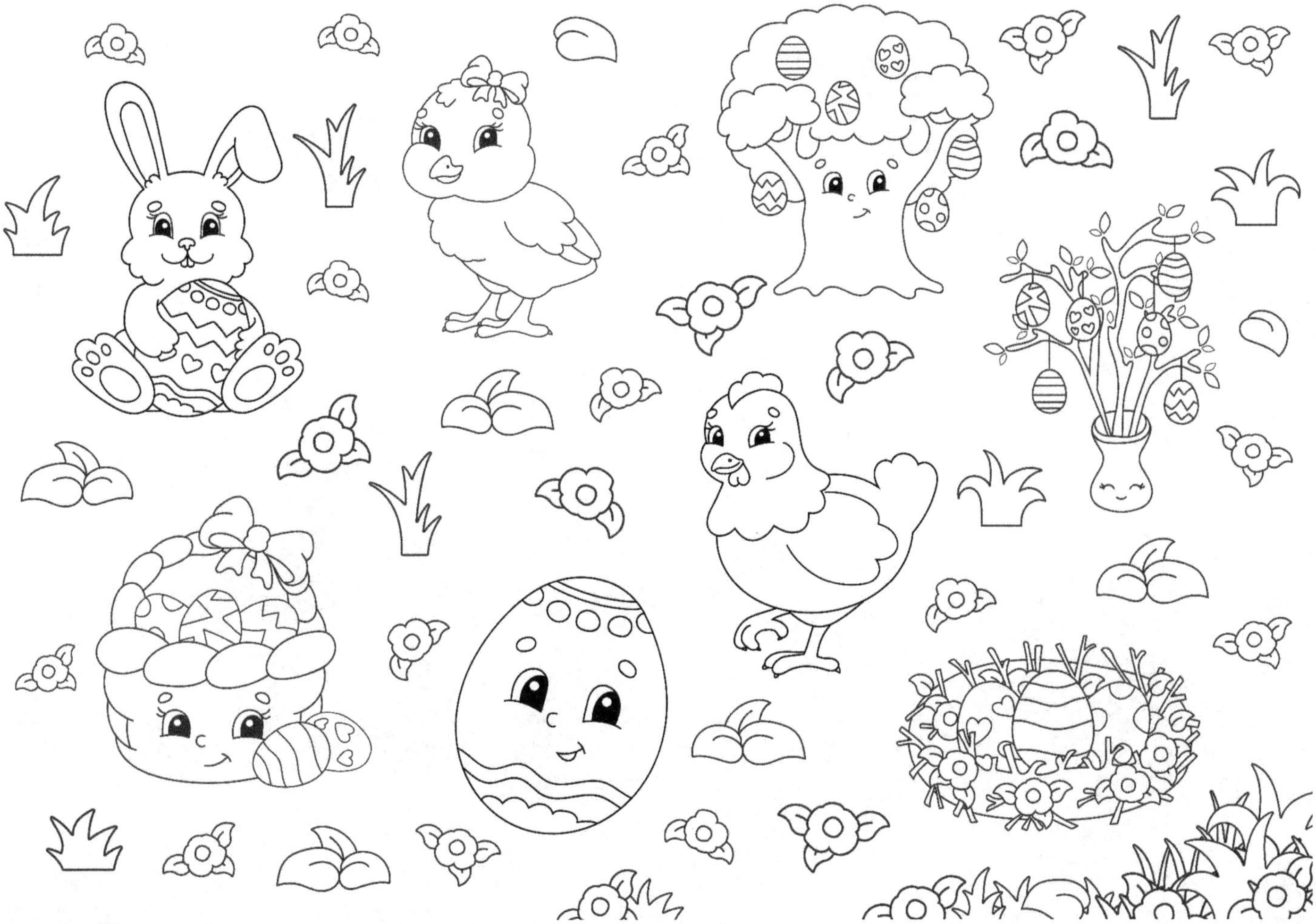

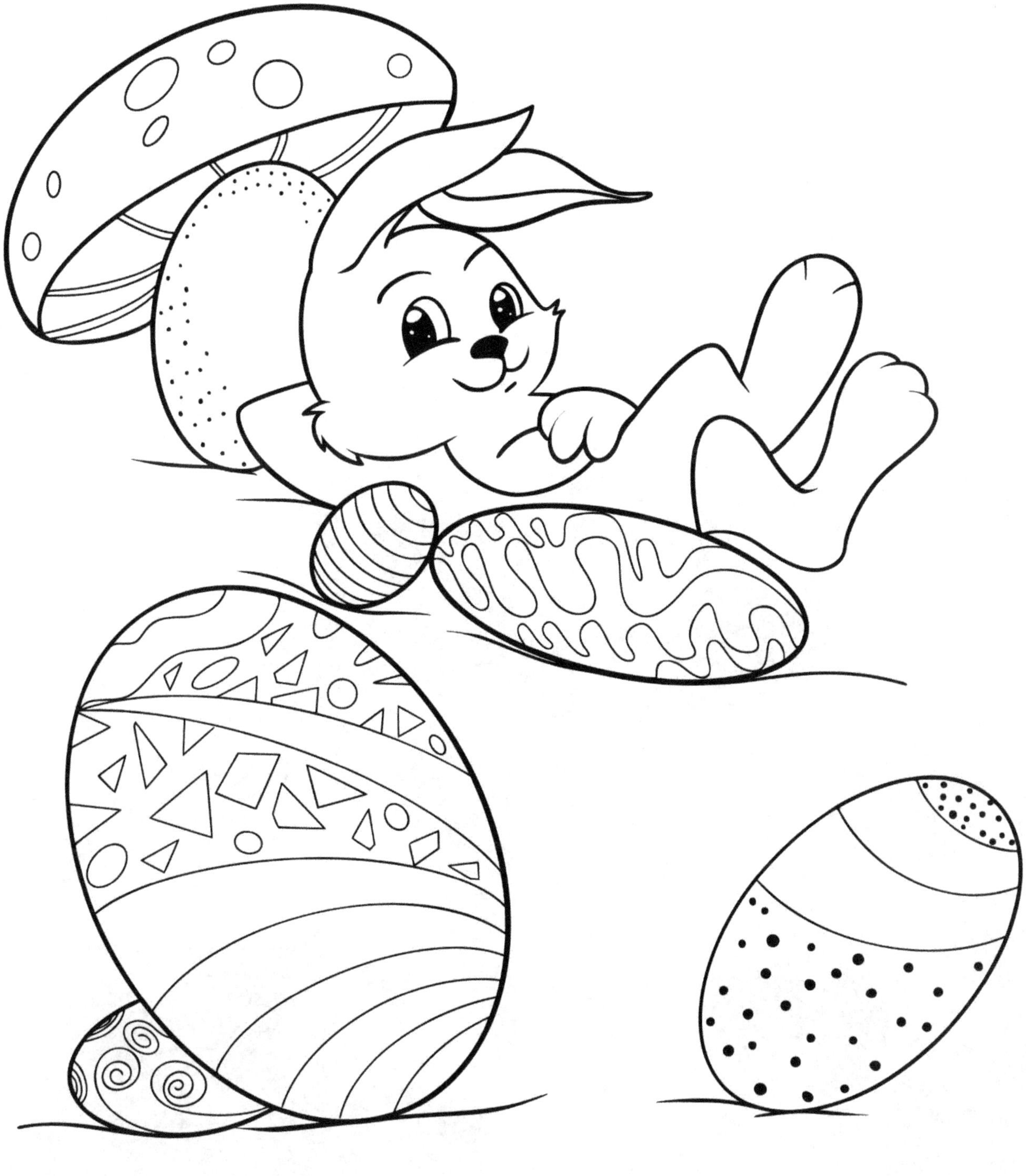

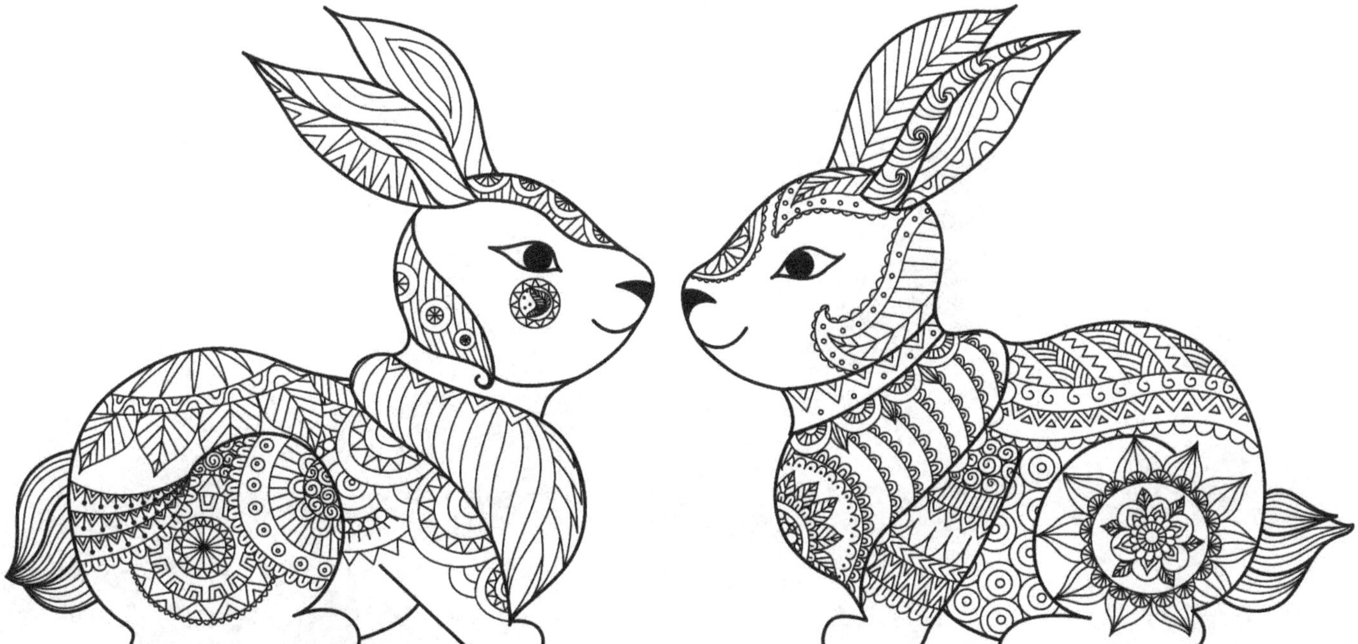

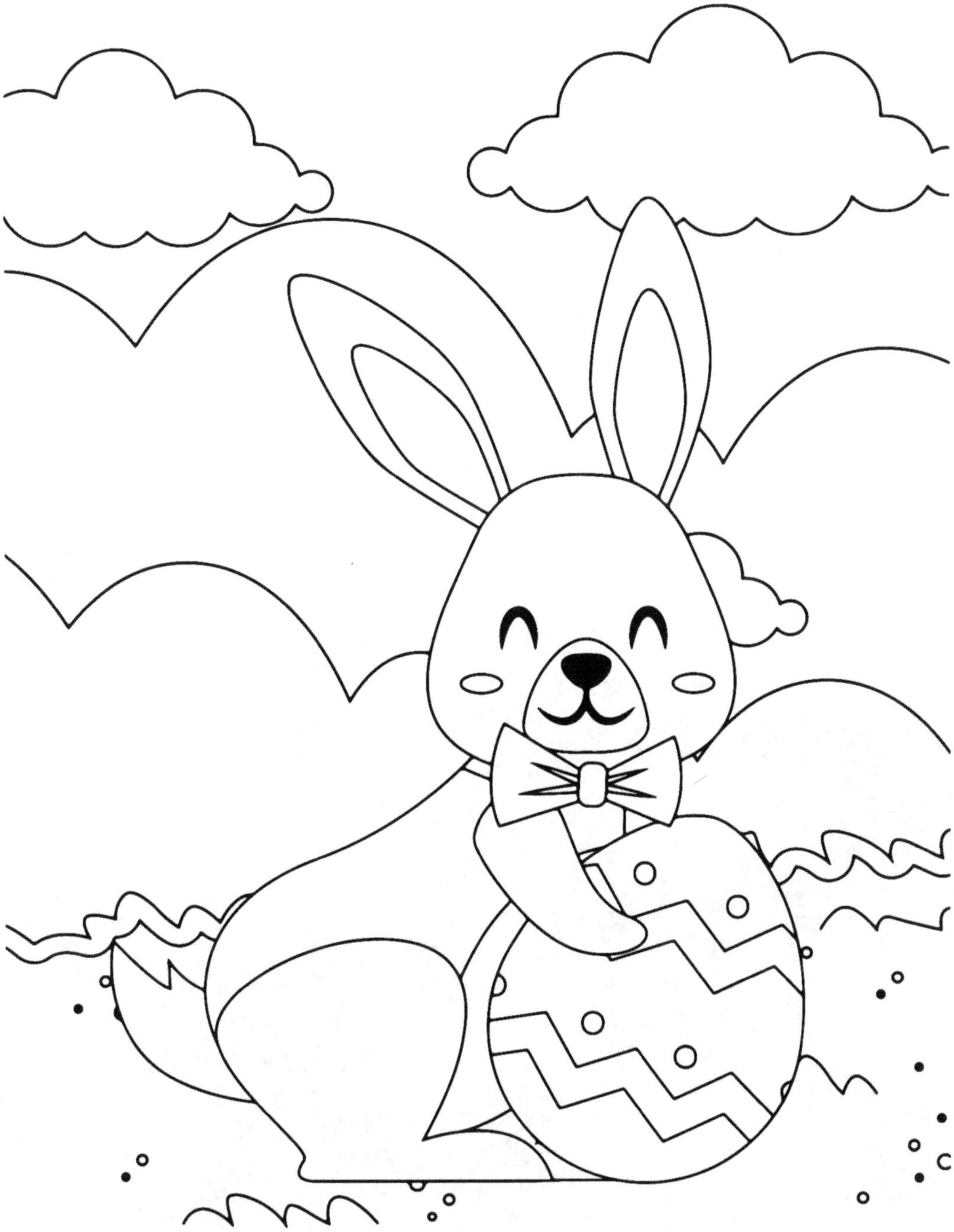

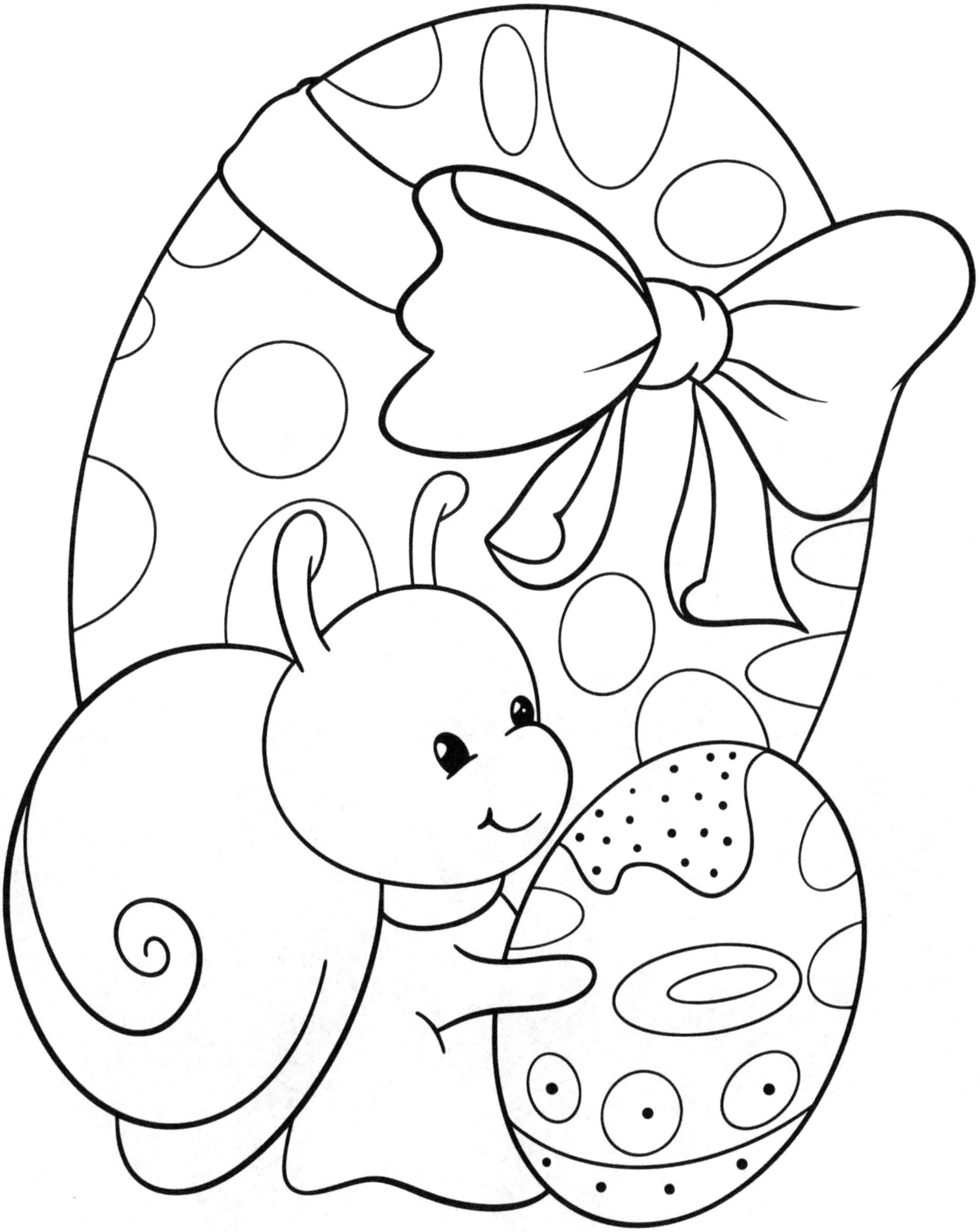

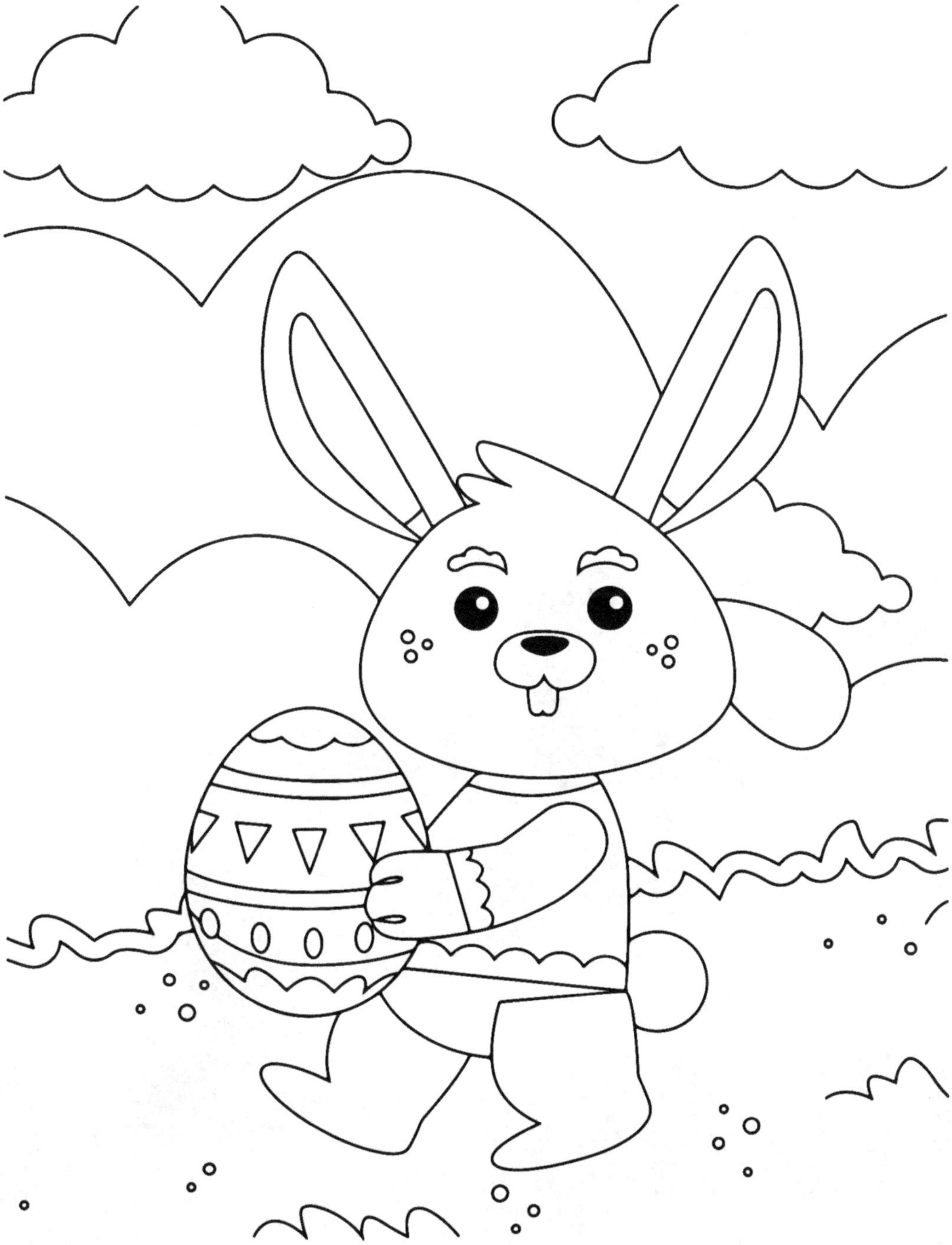

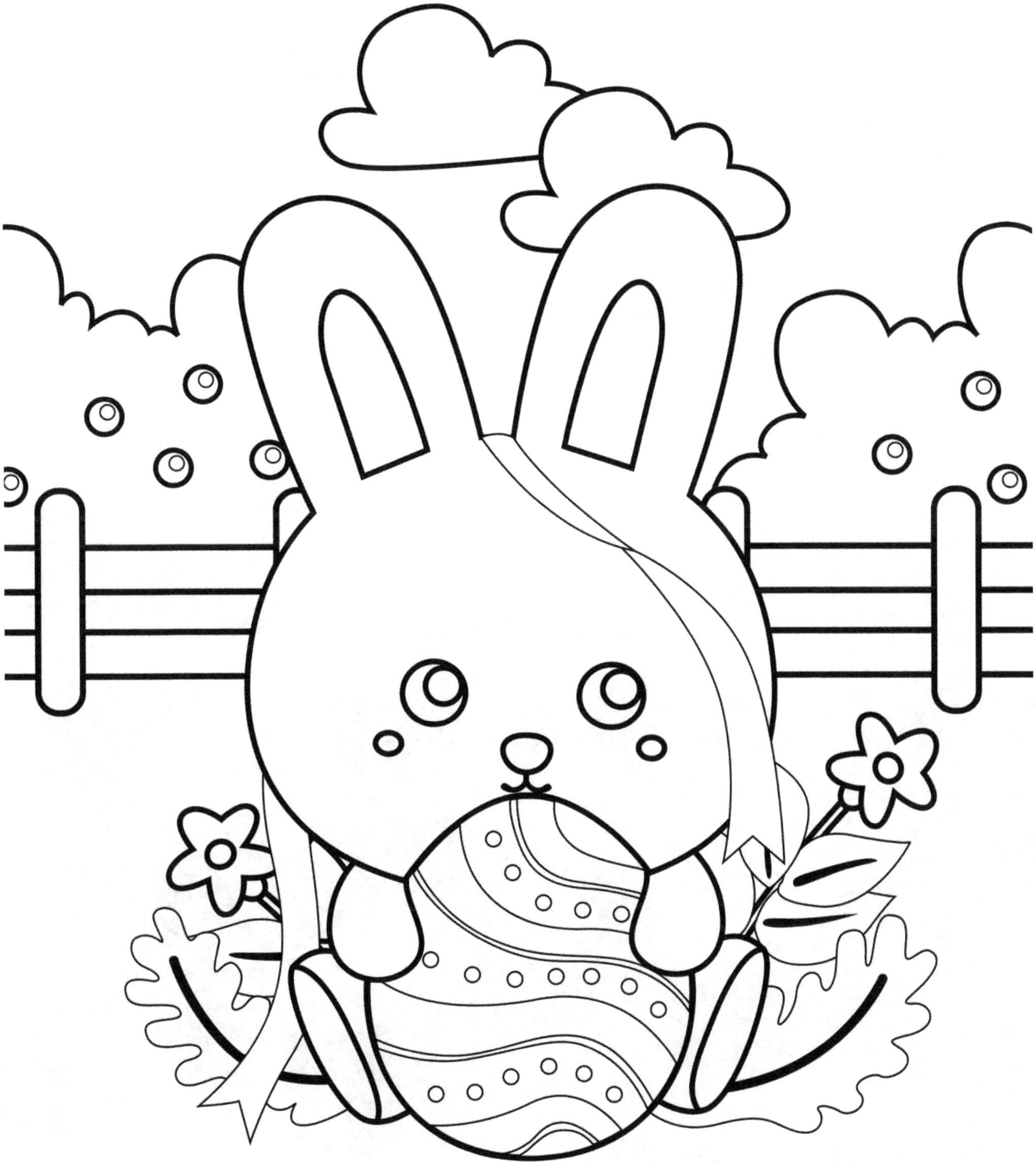

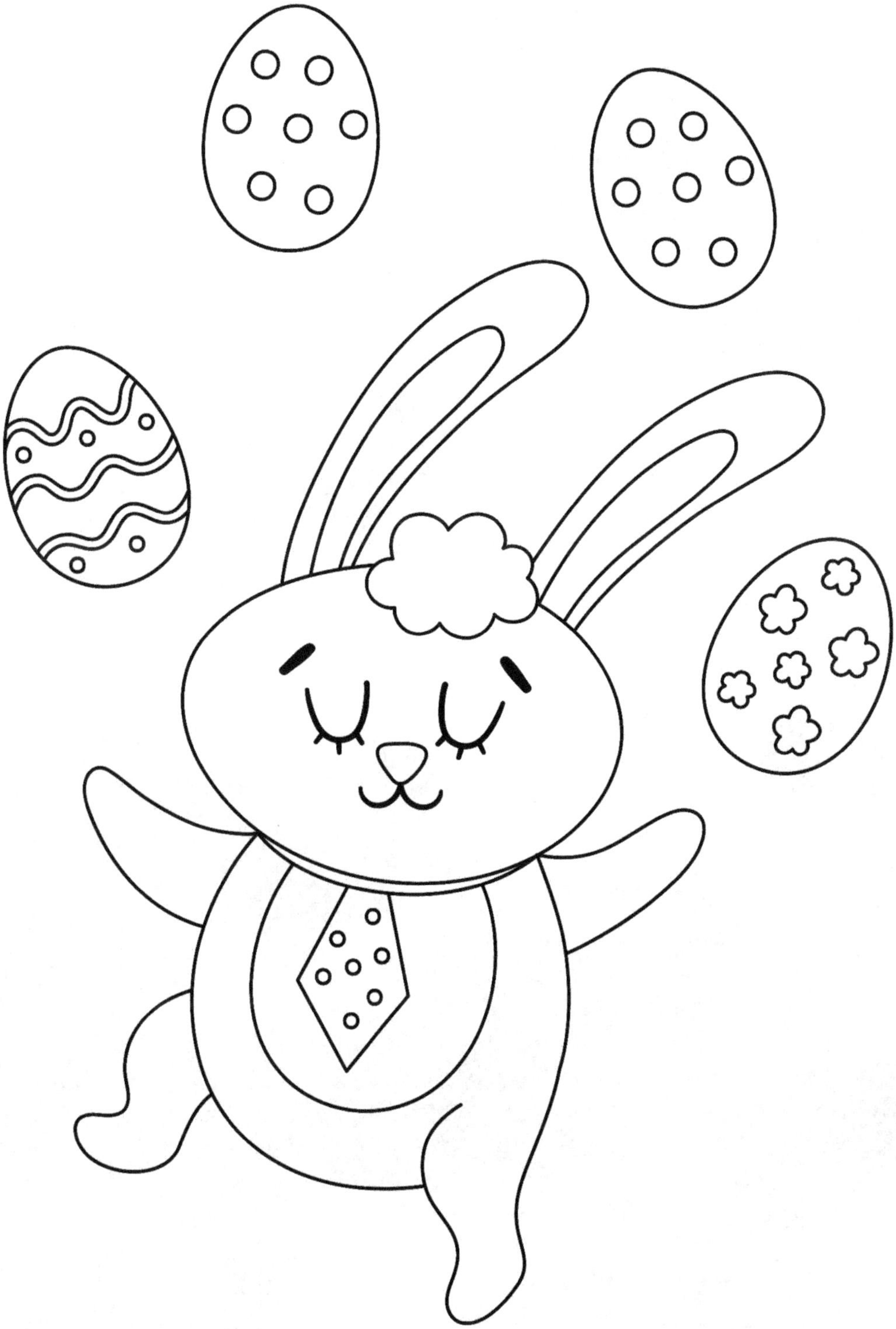

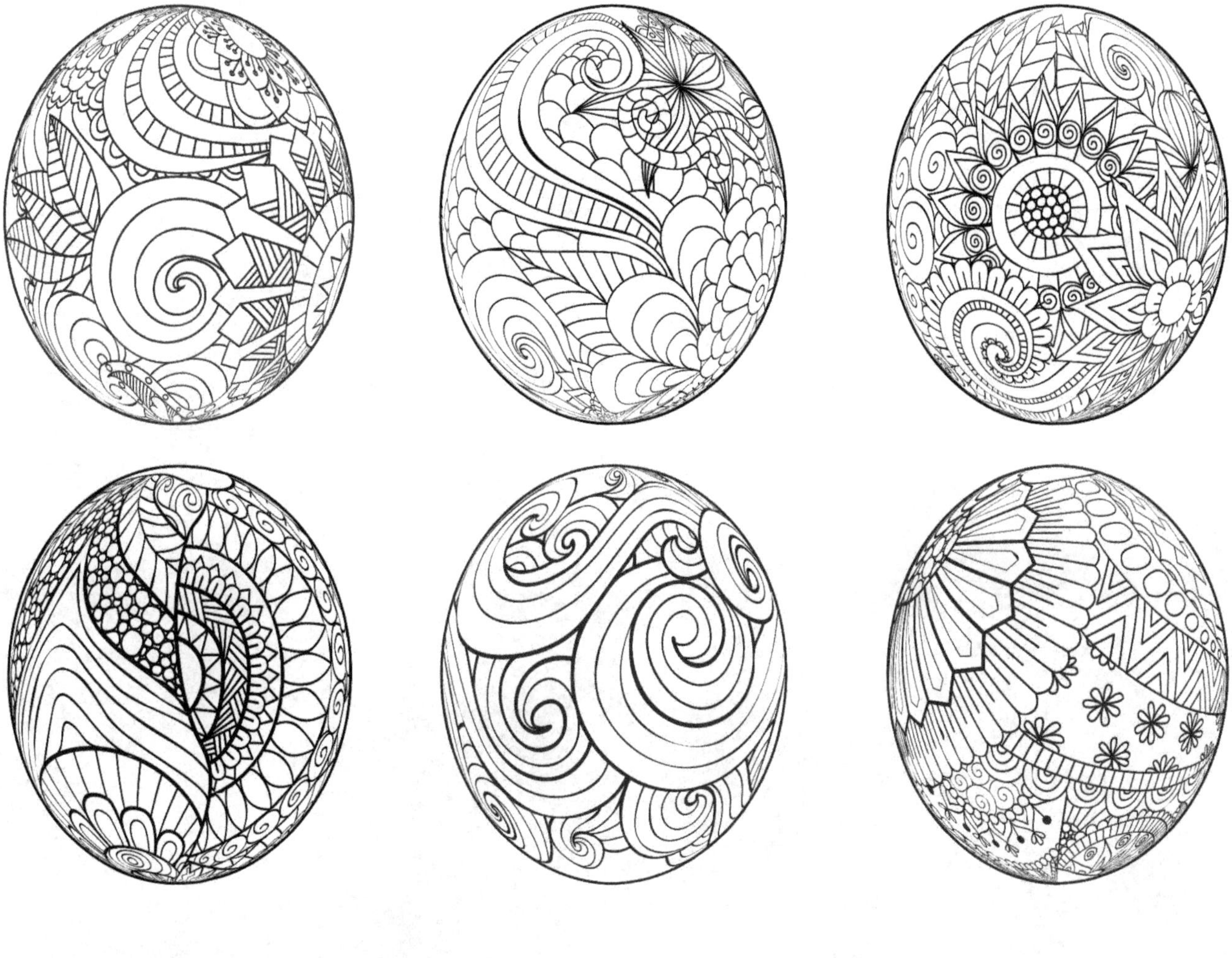

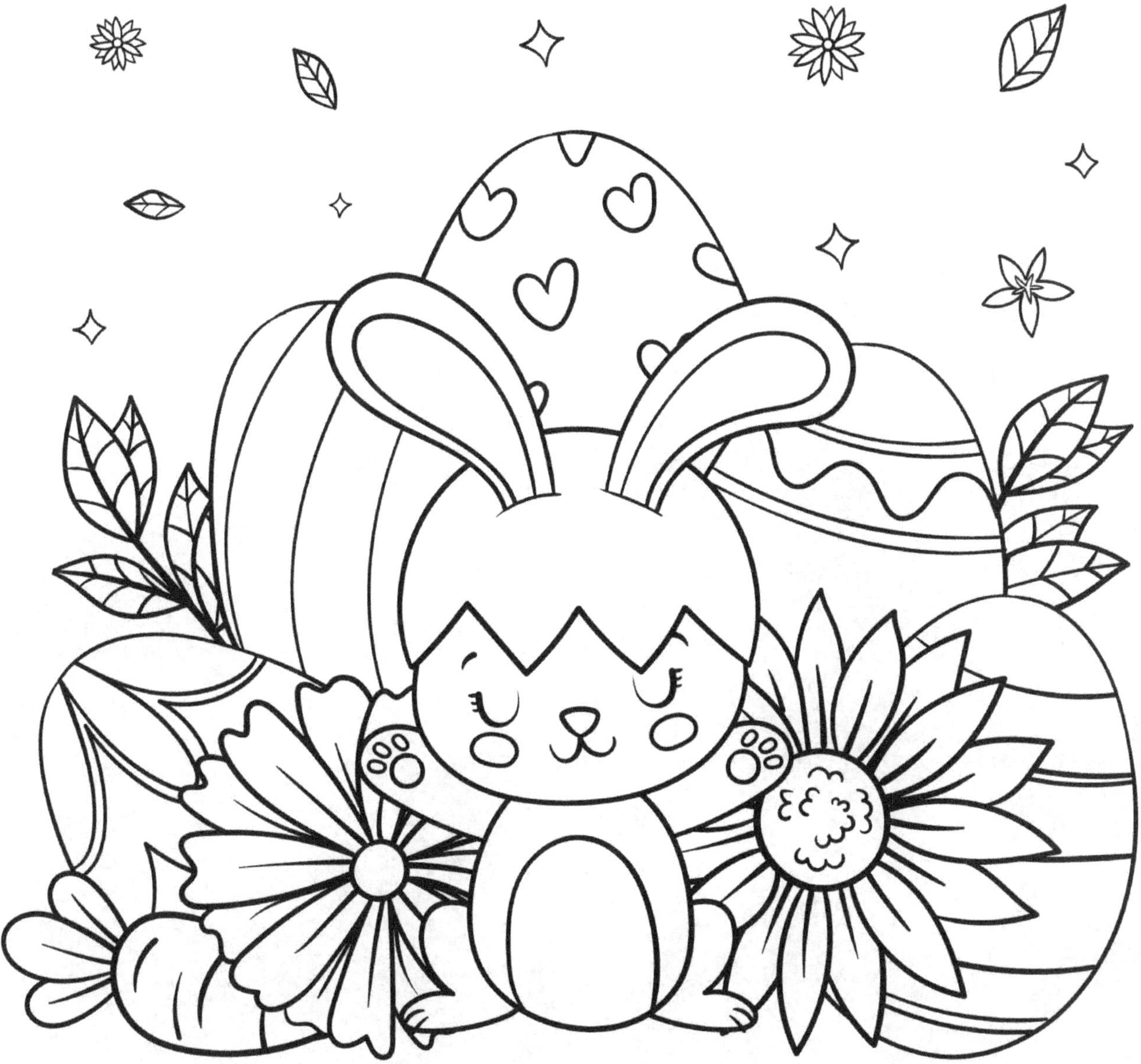

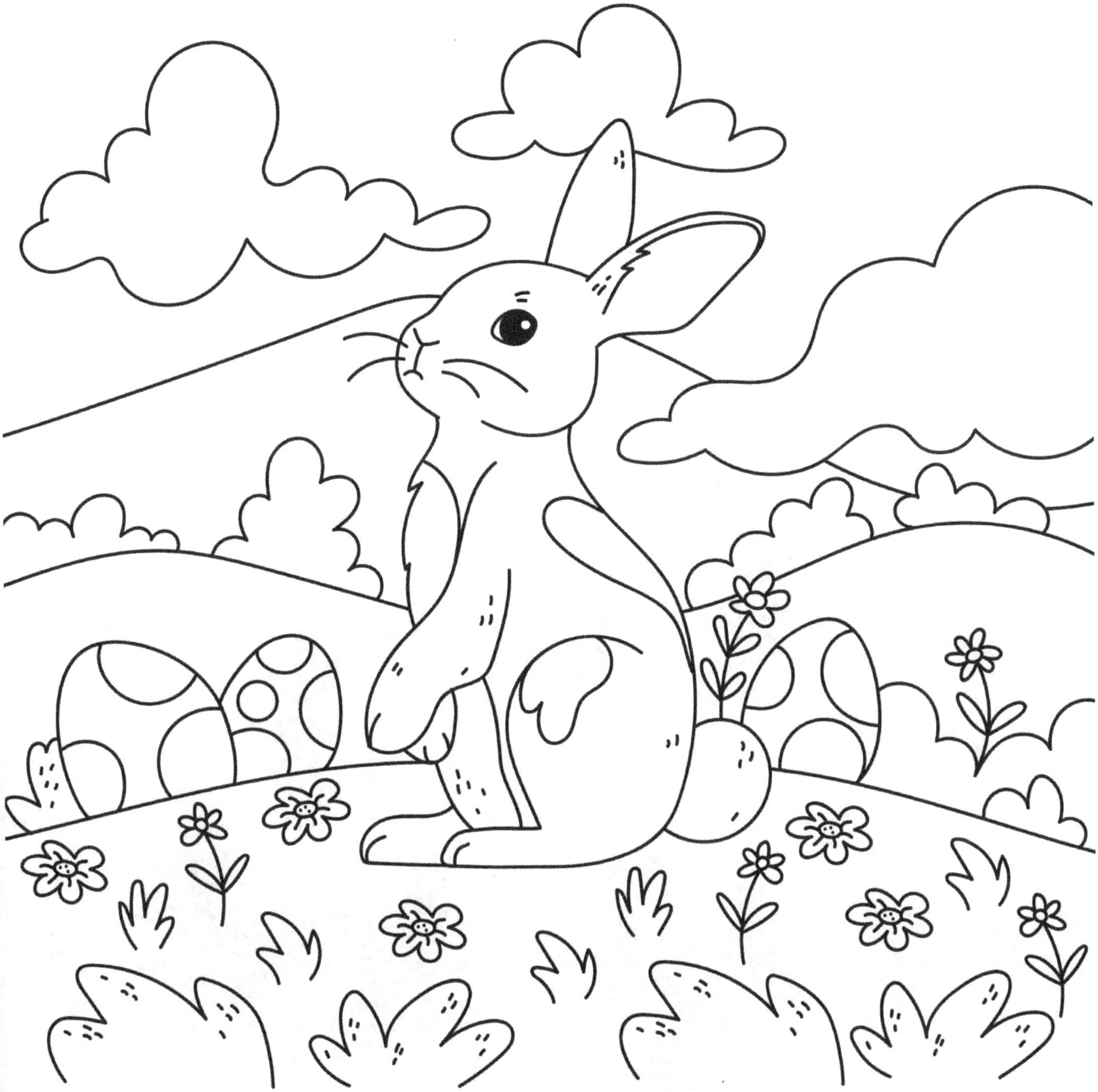

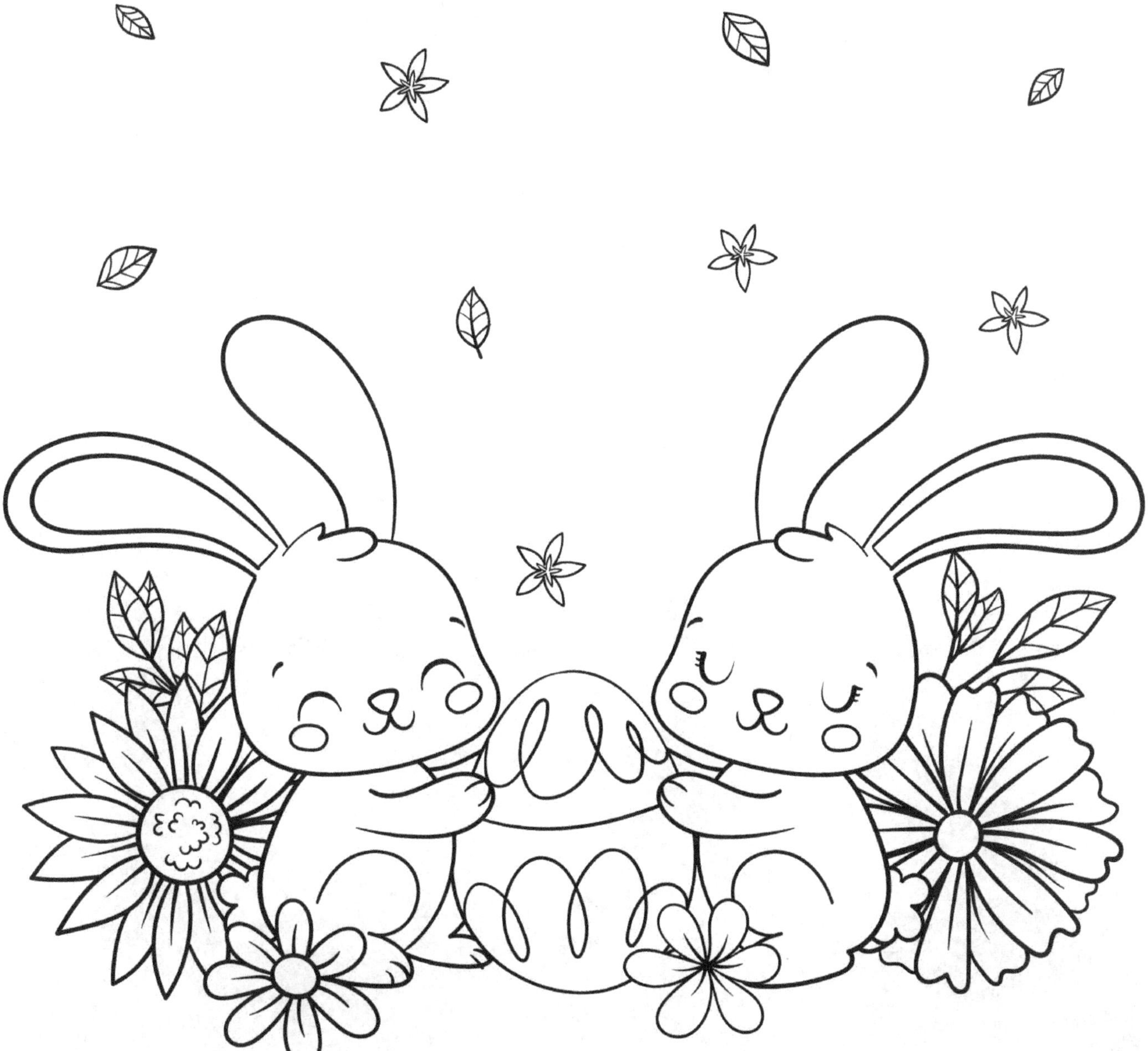

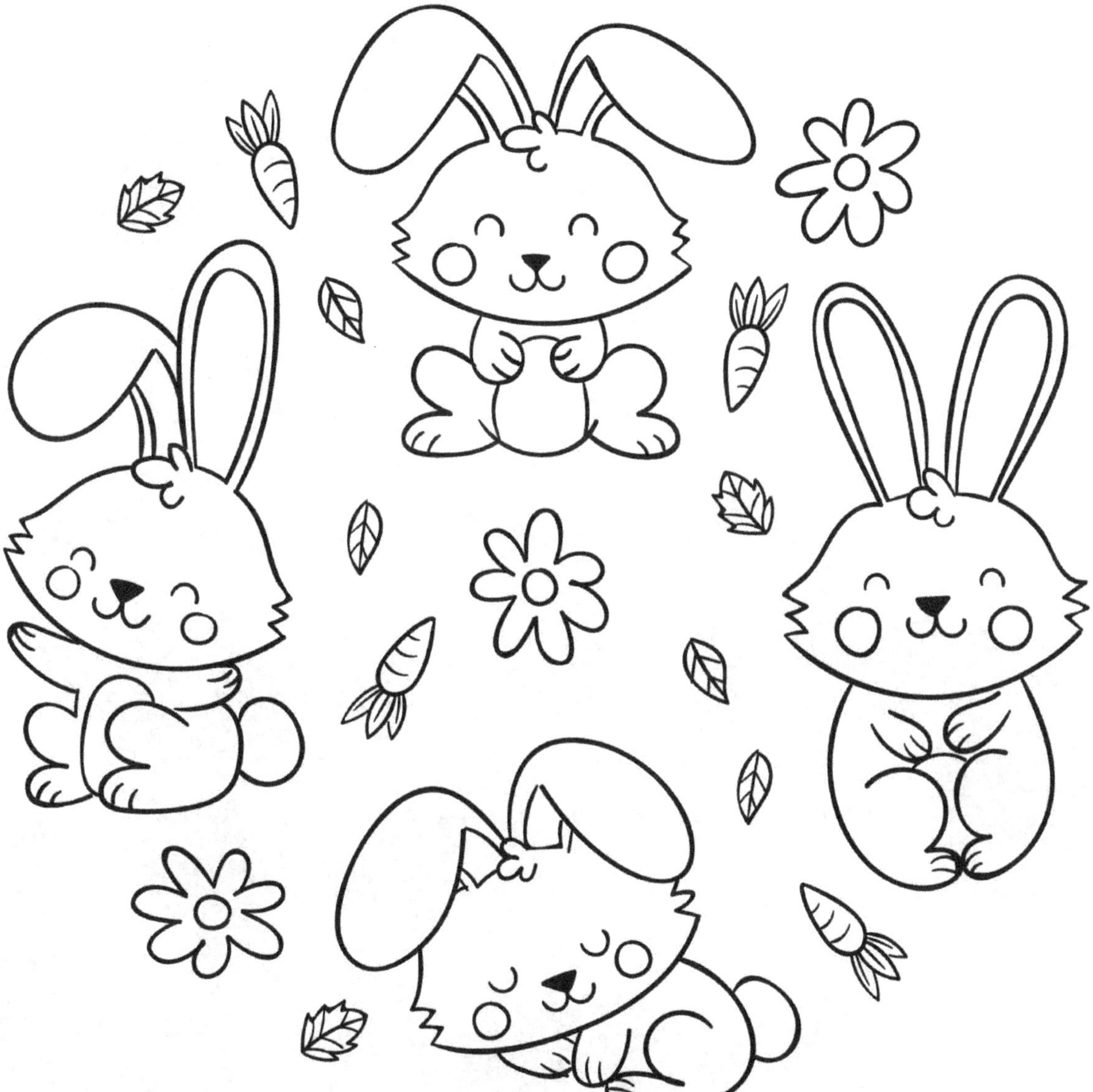

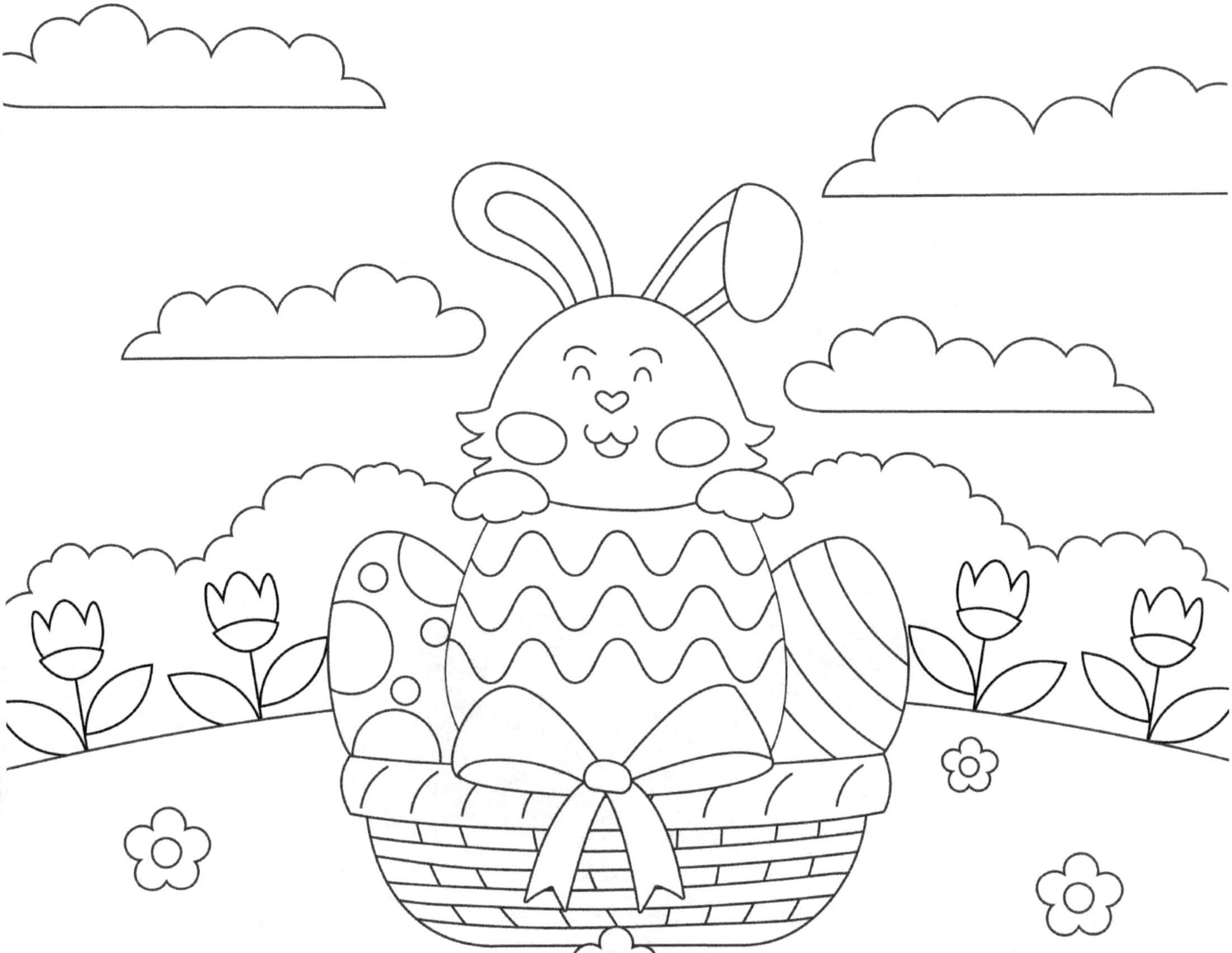

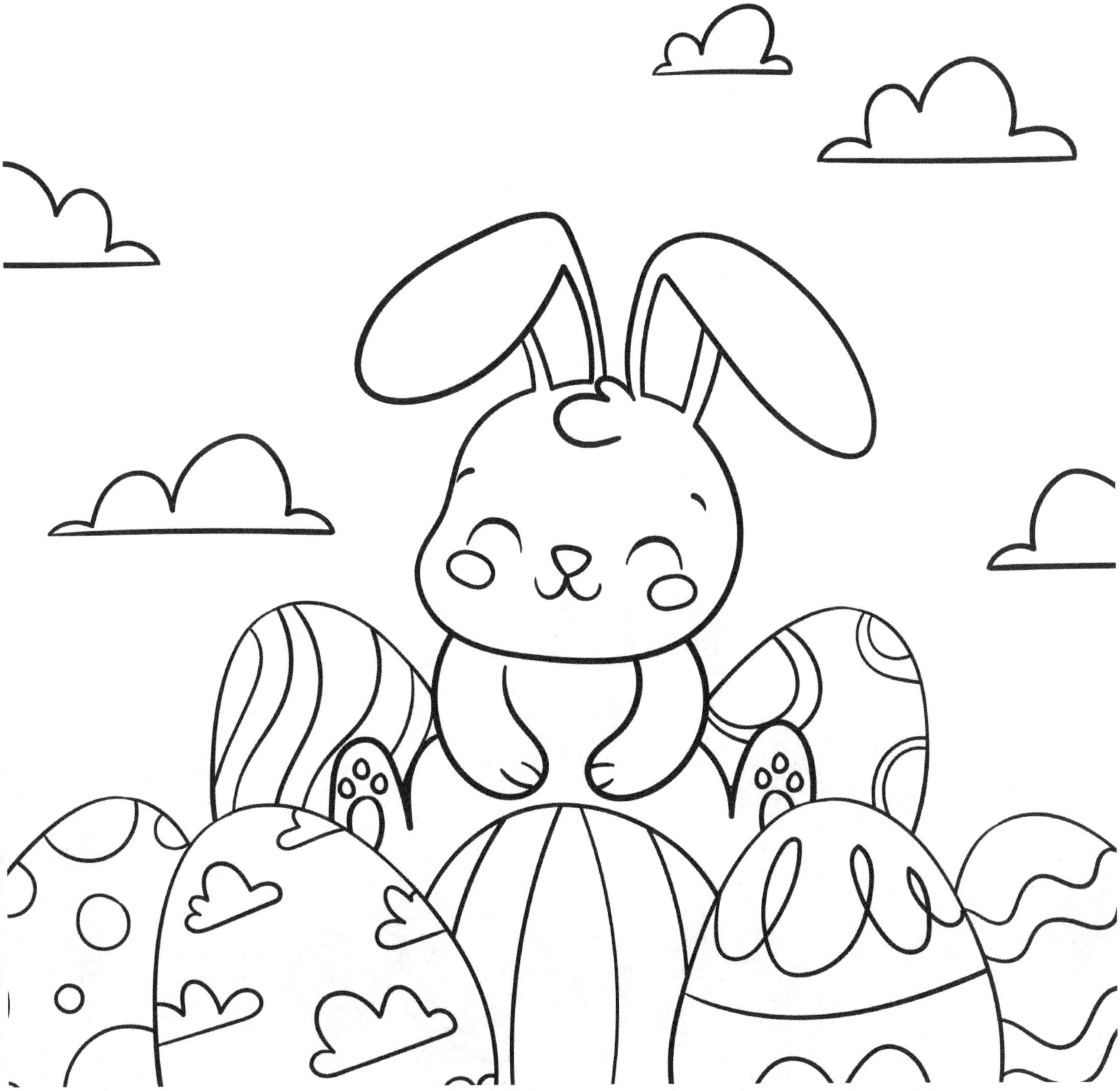

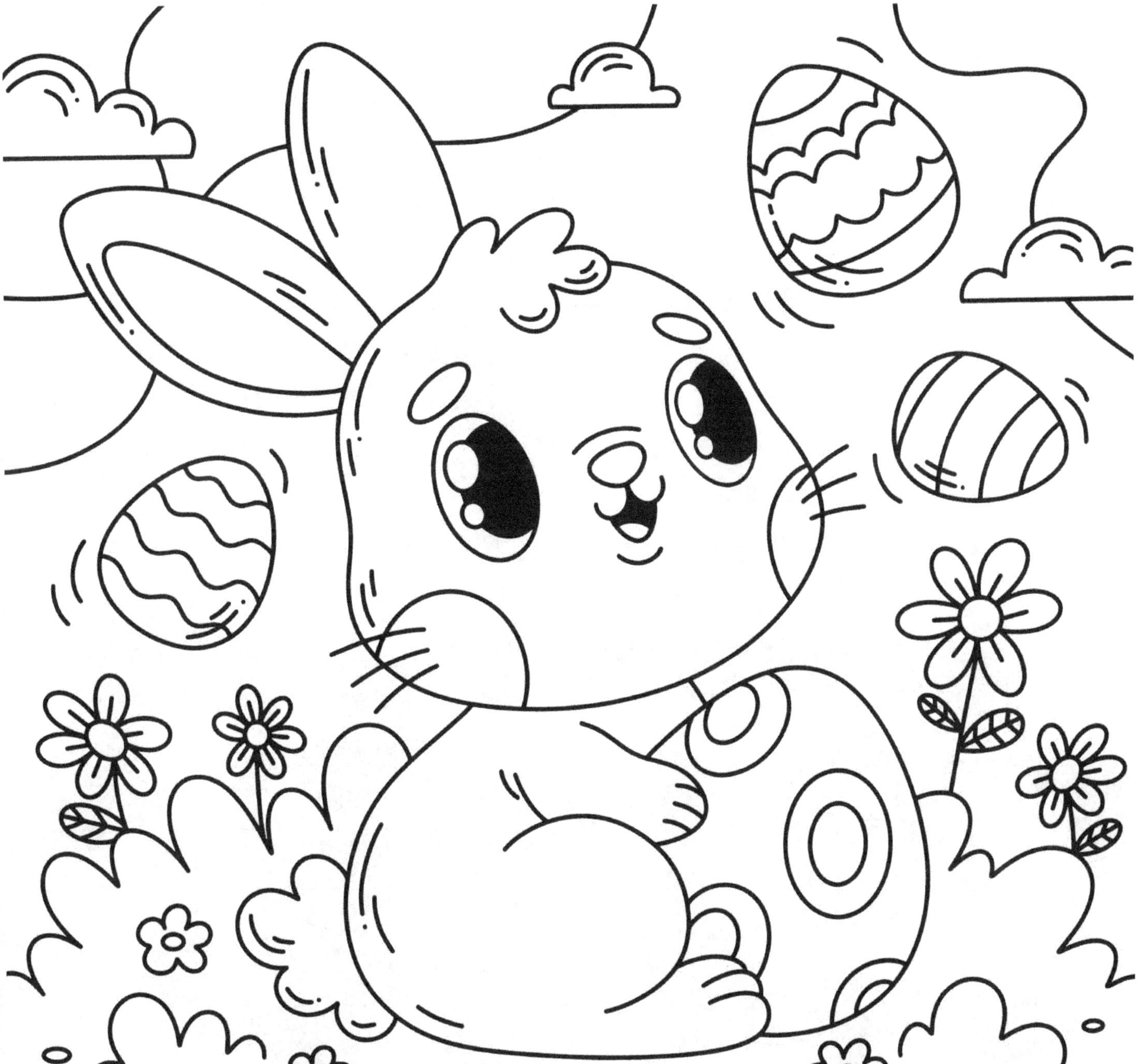

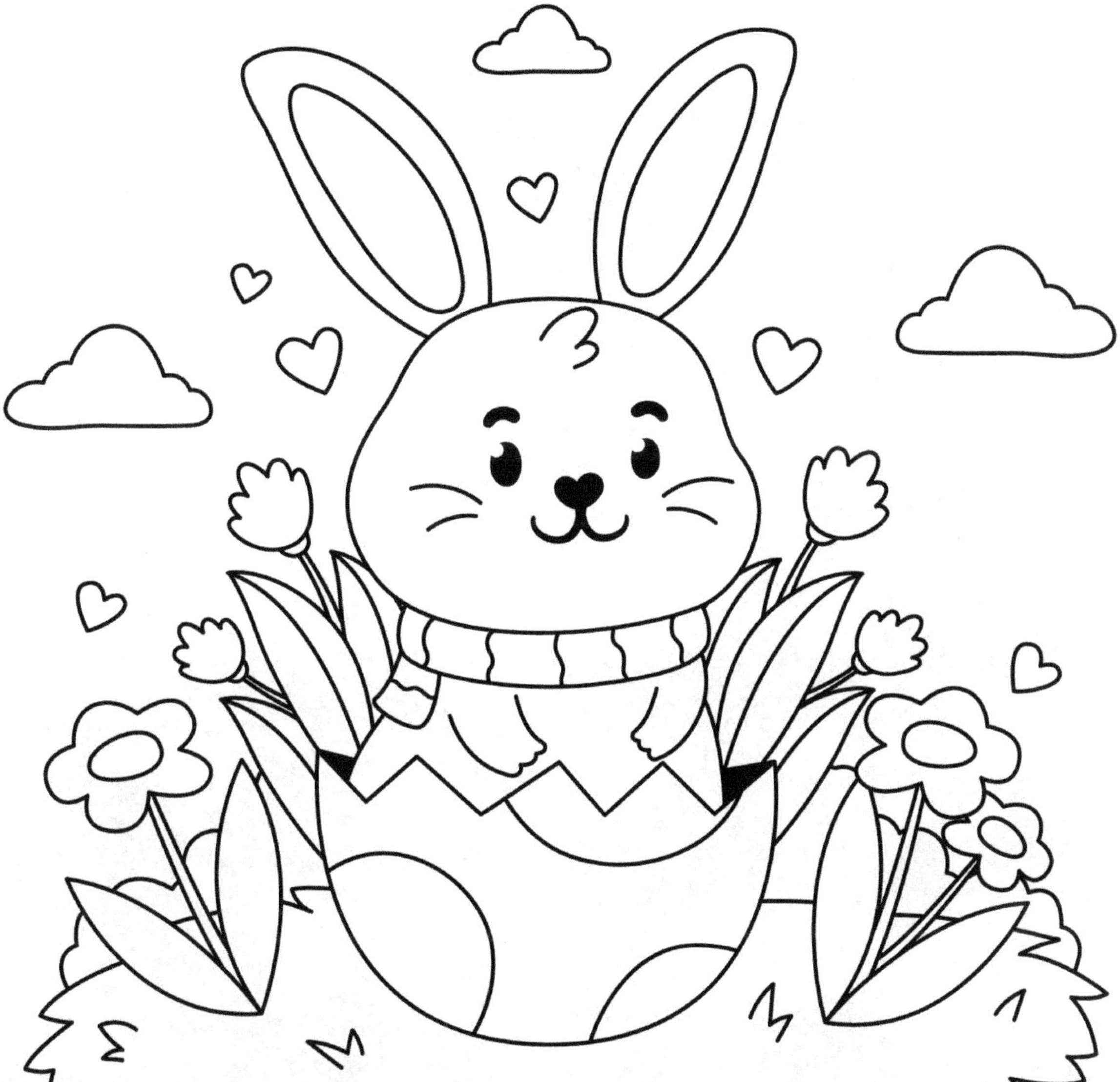

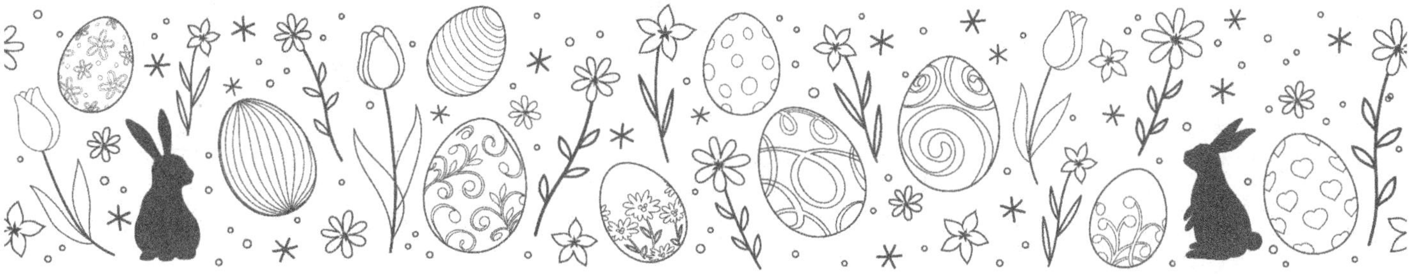

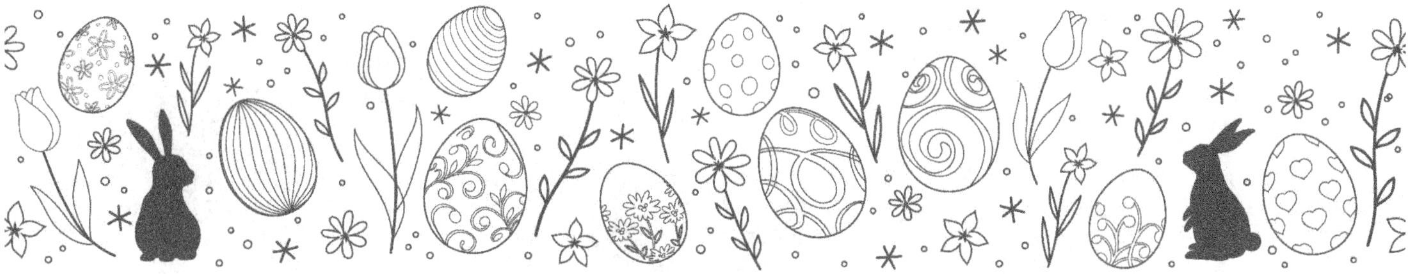

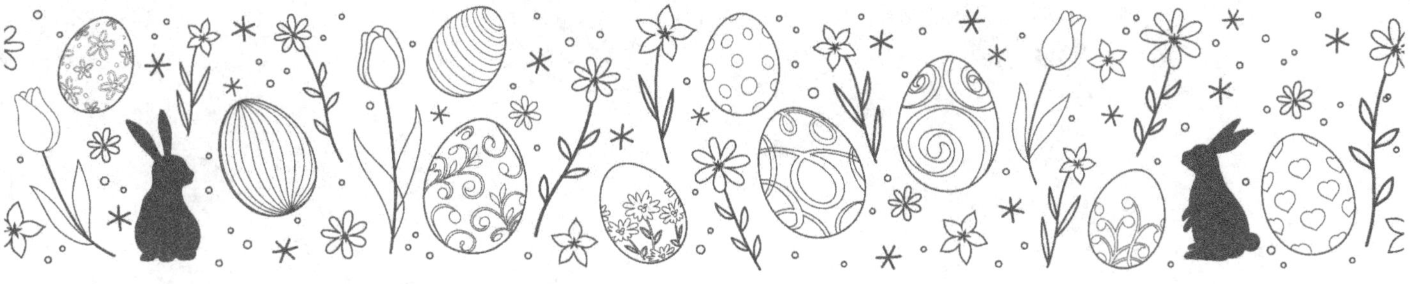

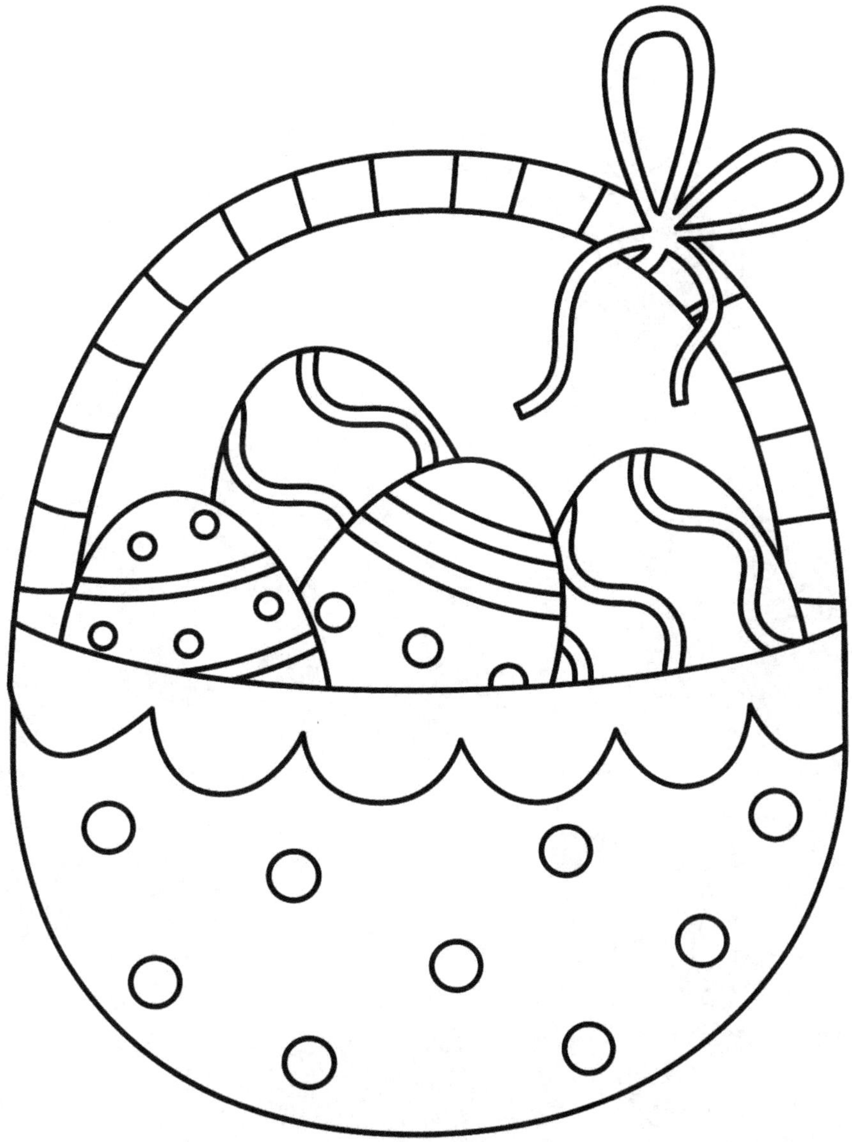

CPSIA information can be obtained
at www.ICGtesting.com
Printed in the USA
LVHW050253060423
743447LV00005BA/117

9 798211 430662